D0870129

Outline of Presentation

I. Caring

   A. Casual conversation
   B. Their church
   C. Our church
   D. Testimony
   E. Dialog questions:
      1. Do you consider yourself to be a Christian?
      2. How does a person become a Christian?

   F. Bridge
      1. A person becomes a Christian through God's free gift.
      2. Becoming a Christian is neither earned nor deserved.

II. Sharing

   A. Every person
      1. Is a sinner
      2. Is born spiritually dead
      3. Is unable to save himself

   B. God
      1. Is just
      2. Is merciful

   C. Christ
      1. Is both God and man
      2. Is our only Savior now and forever

   D. Faith
      1. Is trusting in Jesus Christ alone
      2. Is created by the Spirit through the Word

III. Preparing

   A. Responses
   B. New directions
   C. Follow-up

Who Cares?
A Handbook of Christian Counselling

WHO CARES?
A Handbook of Christian Counselling

by

Evelyn H. Peterson, Ph.D.

Morehouse-Barlow Co., Inc.
Wilton, Connecticut

ISBN: 0-8192-1317-9
Copyright © Evelyn H. Peterson, 1980

First edition published 1980
The Paternoster Press
Paternoster House
3 Mount Radford Crescent
Exeter UK EX2 4JW

First USA edition published 1982
Morehouse-Barlow Co., Inc.
78 Danbury Road
Wilton, Connecticut 06897

Library of Congress Catalog Card Number 82-60447
Printed in the United States of America

In memory of
my parents,
Edwin and Helen Peterson,
who taught the meaning of
loving the Lord
with one's mind

Contents

PART 1
Definition of Christian Counselling

CHAPTER ONE
The Need for Christian Counselling Services

THIS is an age of anxiety. But where does an individual go to get help to understand and cope with his personal agony? The need is urgent. Modern society has increased the personal stress of the individual. There is the increased pressure from without, to conform to the changing standards of the world; and then there is the subtle pressure from within, to analyse one's psyche. This means that in spite of an absence of guidelines for living, the person is still supposed to understand himself.

Personal problems are expected today. Loneliness, meaninglessness, conflicts, addictions, insomnia, uncontrolled anger, hidden anxiety, acute guilt, strange fears, marital stress — these are all accepted as psychological problems. Each of these problems can develop in intensity, to the point where the person becomes trapped, a prisoner of his own problem. It is always possible to pretend that the problems will disappear in time, but when they grow worse instead, some help must be sought. Then a new problem emerges — how to obtain competent counselling.

The person is hurting inside, and needs to be loved. But help cannot come from a superficial professional diagnosis, nor a well-meaning 'pat on the back' approach. Rather there must be a realistic love-in-action approach. The whole person needs to be loved and helped through relevant counselling. It should be a love tempered with enough knowledge to reach the person without increasing the problem. This takes a very special kind of love, shown in a very special type of person.

Where is such love to be found today? Neither this need for love via counselling, nor the demonstration of it in action is new. There is more awareness of the psychological aspects of life now, but Christians have given this kind of help from the start. Historically, the first counselling facilities were at the beginning of the Christian era! Many early Christian monks turned their monastery into a 'psychological city of refuge'. They were places where the problems of men could be met by the healing power of love. Thus, long before the techniques of psychology and/or psychiatry were in vogue, the basic principles of healing through love were applied. Why? Because these early Christians chose to care for the community of man. Genuine caring always leads to counselling, to help the person to help himself and thus become a 'whole' person. As a result of the Christians who cared, those suffering from emotional problems could then choose to get help.

The Christian and Emotional Problems

But there is a new factor today. Many Christians are suffering emotionally, but they must keep quiet about it. This is due to the belief that "Christians should not be emotionally ill." Somehow, it is assumed that one's corrected (redeemed) spiritual nature will automatically maintain a healthy psychological nature too. As a result, signs of emotional distress are interpreted as a spiritual disease called "lack of faith". This leaves the Christian with but two alternatives. Either he must repress reality and the struggle to cope with stress by acting 'normal'; or he must "crack up" emotionally, admit the problem and then end up feeling guilty.

Christians are human beings. Therefore they are vulnerable to physical and/or psychological illness. Physical disease is caused by identifiable factors (e.g. viruses, heredity, age, accidents). The Christian is exposed as much to all of these as is the non-Christian. The same is true of emotional illness. As more and more of the causes of these disorders are known, it will become clear that Christians are exposed to each of these as well.

One such cause is early parental rejection. If a seventeen-year-old girl is forced to marry because she is pregnant, then the child born of this union is likely to be unwanted. A combination of ignorance about the responsibilities of motherhood and rebellion towards her own parents for making her marry, may lead this girl to neglect her own child. From an unwillingness to get up at 4 a.m. to feed a screaming baby, to an inability to know what to do when colic develops, all these behaviours communicate one word to the child — rejection. Or if another couple, this time in their late thirties, decide to have their first child in order to maintain a shaky marriage — this baby may be born into a confused family. Because of better financial resources, these parents may 'give' the child many things but never their love. This is because his presence in the family has made the ongoing marital stress even worse. What they had hoped would strengthen their marriage had failed. Consequently, the child becomes the victim of their increased anger toward each other. Emotionally, the child grows up feeling rejected.

There are many other interacting causes of emotional disorders. Some of these include the following: poor parental models; emotional manipulations via guilt; absence of consistent discipline; standards of perfectionism in behaviour; inability to communicate feelings; emotional hurt producing withdrawal; excessive fantasy to escape reality; avoidance of responsibility and thereby loss of self-respect; fear of commitment producing isolation; mistrust of others and oneself; exaggeration of minor problems into traumas; self-indulgence to compensate for inferiorities; deep feelings of being unlovable; and a continual confusion between reality and non-reality. Any of these causes may combine with a genetic predisposition to specific temperaments.

All these factors relate to the Christian and the unbeliever. Both need counselling. But the love of God may be perceived differently. The non-Christian client will not have accepted and/or understood the reality of God's love, while the Christian client may now be avoiding and/or distorting the power of that love. Both types of clients may find it difficult to believe that God loves them unconditionally. Although the primary emphasis in this book is on how a Christian can best be trained to counsel other Christians, the principles involved would apply also to a Christian ministering to a non-Christian. In either case the counsellor must deal with a problem: that of how and when to present the love of God in Christ to the client. If this is done too soon, it may divert attention from the psychological problems; if this is left too late, the satisfaction of emotional release can also divert the client from seeking any help from

God. This very real concern for a Christian counsellor will be discussed further in Chapter 7.

One way the Church ministers to emotional need is by preaching the Gospel. Faith in Christ offers the individual believer a powerful resource for his own emotional healing. Although each Christian is exposed to sufficient stress to produce any emotional disorder, he also has one asset. Because he has received the love of God, he cannot be unlovable. Once the Christian is convinced that God not only knows him completely, but loves him in spite of his weaknesses/sins, then he has an inner security with which to face himself. The emotional needs are still real, but they should no longer be devastating.

A Christian suffering from depression may doubt everything — including the fact that God still loves him. However, he cannot forget the experience of that love, and the reality of this memory can be a needed corrective to his present feelings. A recent convert, who is an alcoholic, may expect God's love to transform his drinking problem immediately. If this does not occur, then self-pity may combine with anger toward God but even in the midst of this emotional state, the Holy Spirit is still able to convict the alcoholic of his self-pity and restore a sense of hope. This will be a realistic hope, founded in the certainty of God's love and including the patience to learn from his suffering. In these ways, God's love is actively at work in the Christian client. It is the power of Christ within which enables the Christian to judge truth from falsehood and gives assurance and/or correction as needed in the process of healing.

The essence of the Gospel message is reconciliation: of God with man, of man with his fellow men and of man with himself. But psychological problems may prevent the last two aspects of reconciliation from becoming a reality in an individual Christian's life. Therefore, the Church must augment its preaching ministry with a counselling ministry.

The healing of relationships can best be done through a relationship — between a Christian counsellor and client. This is because emotional problems bring with them a distorted view of reality. The client is too close to the situation; he must look at both himself and the problem subjectively. Another pair of eyes may look at the same situation but see it more objectively; thus the counsellor can bring Christian love and truth to bear at the points where they are most needed. The counsellor's objectivity can correct the client's emotional overreactions. The counsellor's wisdom can compensate for his irrational thinking. And the counsellor's understanding can combat his desperate sense of aloneness. For a long time, Christians either ignored the need for a counselling ministry or they referred clients to secular professional help. Christians now realise the urgency of the need within the Church. Many Christians today are being obedient to Christ by ministering to the psychological needs of the person. These are not just the responses of the clergy either. In England today, counselling centres using lay-counsellors are becoming more evident. In the United States, where psychology is more of an established profession, there are even more Christian counselling clinics available. Lay-counsellors, professional therapists and concerned ministers now work together (in both countries) towards the same goal — the psychological health of the person. Counselling help is needed at all levels, not just from "specialists". The Church must learn to care.

The Christian Counsellor's Qualifications

Who then should counsel? Two types of Christians should be avoided. First, no novice is wanted. The counsellor must deal with the depths of emotional distress in another person's life. This can be dangerous to the psychological health of both client and counsellor, especially if the counsellor is not adequately prepared. Such preparation must be both spiritual and psychological. Secondly, not just any 'mature' Christian should counsel. Some Christians, with many years of spiritual experience (not necessarily growth), think they know it all. As a consequence, their spiritual superiority is the very thing which prevents them from learning about the diversity of personality problems. This type of counsellor often gives cliché-like answers to a client's complex problems.

There are basic requirements for an effective Christian counsellor. An attitude of willingness to learn is essential. This would include a growing awareness of one's own emotional needs, the areas of strength and weakness within. If a counsellor does not know himself, how can he help another person to know himself? This growing self-knowledge in the counsellor should lead to an emotionally balanced life. He can then genuinely care for others, in a responsible yet unselfish way.

The more the counsellor becomes a channel for the love of God, the easier it is to communicate these essential qualities to the distraught client. But in order to be such a channel, a connection must be maintained to the Source of love — in God. This is never automatic. One of the Holy Spirit's purposes is to guide the Christian into all truth (John 16:13). He is the Teacher, but the Christian may be too insensitive to his voice to be learning. Perhaps some spiritual rebellion and/or psychological conflict is jamming the circuit of communication to the believer. Or theologically poor teaching on the person of the Holy Spirit may prevent the Christian from seeking the gift of discernment. Without this discernment, a counselling ministry can become too dependent upon knowledge only.

The Holy Spirit is necessary, but so is knowledge. A mind trained to think is one way of expressing love to God (Mark 12:30). A mind renewed in knowledge can submit to God's will (Romans 12:1-2). But knowledge always implies learning.

Many Christians are afraid to counsel because they recognise their own ignorance. Some even mistrust psychological 'knowledge' and, without prior examination of it, assume it must be alien to Christian beliefs. But since Christ is the source of all truth (John 14:6), any proven psychological insight must agree with scriptural truth. Relevant knowledge of human behaviour affects the emotional maturity of the counsellor as well. The scripture states that "a man of knowledge uses words with restraint, and a man of understanding is even-tempered" (Proverbs 17:27).

Spiritually, the individual Christian must be prepared to counsel via a daily submission to the Holy Spirit; psychologically, the Christian must be trained via a learning of relevant principles of behaviour. This dual preparation will allow God's blessing to be applied to this demanding ministry.

This book is for people who want to be prepared for a counselling ministry. It explains some reasons why people need counselling. It outlines the underlying causes of the major psychological disorders. It explains basic methods of counselling. Because it is written primarily for Christians, it has another dimension. It shows how the Gospel, experienced through Christian fellowship, can meet emotional needs. But this happens only when the Church chooses to care. When the individual Christian sees the need for this ministry of caring, then he must be trained for it.

Reading this book will not make a Christian into a counsellor. That is the job of the Holy Spirit. But it can be one of the many means used by God to prepare his people for a ministry of caring. Christians who are called to such a ministry can use it as a basic textbook. Churches who are setting up a counselling service can use it to train their counsellors. "To bind up the broken-hearted, . . . to provide for those who grieve in Zion" — this can then be the reality of a Church which cares.

Points for Discussion

1   Why might a Christian need competent counselling?
    Why might it be more difficult for a Christian to obtain this service?

2   What are some of the 'masks' that Christians wear to cover up their psychological problems?

3   Look at the list of the possible causes of emotional disorders. Which ones do you think are more likely to produce problems within a Christian client?

4   In what way may counselling be an opportunity for evangelism?
    What are the dangers of this?

5   How may the fact that a client is a Christian be a help in coping with stress?

6   Why is it often necessary to involve a counsellor in an emotional problem rather than trying to sort it out oneself? *subj vs. obj.*

7   How may different people within the Church all work together to minister to the psychological needs of the person? *lay / therapist / minister*

8   What is the interaction of knowledge and discernment in Christian counselling?

CHAPTER TWO

The Goals of the Counselling Process

Definition of Counselling

COUNSELLING is essentially communication. But it is communication with a specific purpose: counselling is communication that seeks to heal emotional hurts. This healing occurs within the relationship developed between two people — the counsellor and client. A more complete definition would be as follows: counselling is the process of communicating understanding, respect and helpfulness to a client.

First of all, counselling is a *process*. Apart from crisis intervention work, counselling generally takes time to achieve specific goals. Healing itself is a process, and the length of time it requires will depend on the depth of hurt, both its intensity and its duration. During the time needed for counselling, repressed emotions and memories may surface, and destructive thinking patterns can be unlearned. Sometimes there may be a moment of sudden insight, but time is still needed to integrate a new aspect of oneself into the old distorted self-concept. There are often 'dry' periods in counselling when outwardly no progress is seen, and these demand patience on the part of the counsellor and perseverance from the client. External signs of healing may bring encouragement, but these are often just precursors of the deeper healing that may be less dramatic. The client who feels distressed, often when change comes slowly, will need encouragement to continue a counselling relationship in spite of recurring symptoms.

Counselling means *communication*. Communication always continues on several levels simultaneously, and each level or channel must be accurately perceived. The two most basic channels are the verbal and the non-verbal. In verbal communication, words convey ideas, but the tone in which they are spoken also reveals motives and emotions. In counselling, the client may be focussing most on his words, yet it is his motives/emotions that will show more of the real problem. If the counsellor picks up this motivation from the client's intonation and pauses in speech, then this becomes the first step toward unravelling the emotional chaos.

But the counsellor must also be aware of non-verbal factors. For example, how the client is dressed, the pattern of bodily movement, the degree of eye contact, the physical signs of anxiety in facial muscles, or of anger in clenched fists — all speak louder than words alone. Contradictions between the verbal and non-verbal channels often indicate a more serious problem. Thus, if a woman verbally complains (with tears) of her feelings of helplessness in a depression, yet is dressed like a model, what she is saying is contradicted by how she chose to dress. This means that this client's self-concept is distorted, which may be more serious than her depression. If a husband boasts of his non-involvement with another woman, yet shifts his eye contact and twitches his hands at each mention of her name, the non-verbal channel is communicating a sense of guilt within him. This is the psychological rule: speech often maintains the self-deceptions of the client, but non-verbal behaviour unmasks them. By picking up these non-verbal cues, the counsellor can gain much truth which can then be used to heal the person.

If counselling is to produce healing, then *understanding* must be communicated to the client. Indeed, this is the essence of healing: to feel understood means that another has broken into the privacy of one's psyche. As long as the client experiences aloneness, the intensity of his problems are increased. Fears unshared become phobias; hidden anxieties are exaggerated into panic states; unconfessed guilt demands unreasonable punishment; and uncorrected self-images become monstrous self-distortions. In a healthy personality, an honest sharing of oneself can prevent deep emotional hurts; while in a diseased one, it can help to heal them. However, the counsellor must remember that understanding does not mean agreement. To communicate understanding of the client's distress is not the same as condoning his motives and/or behaviour. One can understand the hatred felt toward a cruel parent during childhood, but strongly disagree with the revengeful behaviour in the client's relationship to that parent now. Often, in fact, the client cannot condone his feelings to himself; just to be understood by another is enough.

Respect must also be communicated to the client in counselling. Since emotional hurts erode self-confidence, many clients come with both real problems and real self-hatred. They may expect to be hurt within the counselling relationship just as they would expect to be by any relationship in life. To compensate for these hatreds, the counsellor must communicate a sense of intrinsic worth. The ways of doing this are legion. Genuine politeness develops self-respect, as does asking rather than demanding information. Listening without seeming pressured for time conveys the idea that the client is the most important person to the counsellor at that moment. The client's right to withhold or to distort data deliberately should be acknowledged openly. No other person, such as a family member, employer, or doctor, should be contacted for additional information unless permission is given by the client first. In a counselling relationship, trust must be earned. When a client cannot trust himself, it is especially difficult to trust another without some basis for believing in that person. Perhaps the client will test the trustworthiness of his counsellor by giving some "shocking" data to determine how much confidentiality will be maintained. If the client's confidences are violated, whatever trust existed will be destroyed and with it the counselling relationship. The counsellor's respect for the client evokes the client's response of trust in the counsellor; both are necessary for counselling to be effective.

Finally, the client must experience the counsellor as *helpful,* able to do and/or say something to alleviate the current distress. Certainly it is important to create hope in the possibility of future change, but some concrete help is required in the immediate situation. Just to assure the client that the counsellor cares and will remain available for other contacts is itself helpful. Sometimes a client is so overwhelmed by hopelessness that emergency measures may be needed. The counsellor may offer to contact the client's family (with his permission), or arrange, if necessary, to provide a weekend away from the stressful situation. But the counsellor's zeal to prove helpful must not lead him to make promises that cannot be kept. Such false promises destroy the counselling relationship.

Some clients may take advantage of this spirit of helpfulness, but it is nonetheless essential for healing. Limitations will safeguard its use. For example, a client should never be given money, no matter how "helpful" this might appear to be. It is better to offer an opportunity to have a meal together, or to earn money in some way.

All of these dimensions of counselling have something in common: in every aspect the counsellor must be able to subordinate himself to the well-being of the client. This is not easy. Most clients, because of their distress, behave in a selfish and demanding manner; but the counsellor must be unselfish and available, through the inward experience of God's love.

Directive versus Non-directive Counselling Approaches

There is no single "best" way of communicating understanding via counselling. The counsellor who adopts a variety of approaches is then able to select the method appropriate for a specific client. But to do this the counsellor must first know something of the different methods available.

It is not within the scope of this book to examine the various techniques used by professional psychotherapists, but it is important for the Christian counsellor to realise that there are two major approaches to counselling in use. The first is the Directive method, based upon Reality Therapy; the second is the Non-directive or Rogerian approach. Each of these theories of counselling has a distinct premise, procedure and limitation.

Directive counselling is the 'hard' approach. It stresses the responsibility of the counsellor to assess and then advise the client regarding his problems. The *premise* is that the counsellor must control and/or direct the counselling sessions. But this can only be done through an involvement with the client. As advice is given in the context of genuine caring for the client — then he is able to admit his need and accept the direction of the counsellor. This method is an application of Reality Therapy as formulated by William Glasser (1965). Reality is interpreted by Glasser as an awareness of the needs of the self which must be fulfilled within the rules of society. Thus to fulfil these needs is to act responsibly (mental health); to deny these needs or the needs of reality is to act irresponsibly (mental illness). The client is by definition irresponsible in behaviour, and it is the goal of the counselling process to teach responsibility. The client must learn how to fulfil his two basic needs — to love and be loved and to feel worthwhile. But this learning must occur within the framework of reality not fantasy. The overworked executive who develops an ulcer, the delinquent teenager who steals cars, or the psychotic patient who experiences hallucinations — each one denies the rules of reality and is irresponsible. By contrast, a responsible person does that which gives him a feeling of self-worth and self-worth is learned by obedience to the moral laws of society (rules of reality). As the client begins to act responsibly, he develops self-worth.

Three words summarise the *procedure* of directive counselling: confrontation, challenge and condemnation. Each violation of reality, such as an immoral thought or an illegal act, is confronted as wrong. The client is not allowed to excuse such behaviour by blaming parents, society or God. On the contrary, he is responsible for his own problems. Logic is then used to challenge the client into changing his behaviour, e.g. to act responsibly. For example, if a client threatens suicide, he is told logically, "We can't help you if you kill yourself." Or if another client continues to act out sexually, the challenge comes in the question, "If it is wrong for your teenage daughter to be promiscuous, is it not also wrong for yourself?" The counsellor must point out the consequences of each irresponsible act, and condemn it as a denial of a moral law (promiscuity) or a legal code (shop-lifting). Because the counsellor cares for the client, he is able to condemn. Because the client knows someone cares, he is able to accept the condemnation, admit his guilt and receive the support of the counsellor to develop enough self-respect to live responsibly.

Directive counselling does not always work. Certain circumstances prohibit it. This method should be avoided whenever the personality of the client is unable to accept authority. Some people become so angry when told what to do that they do the opposite. Certainly, this rebellious nature is potentially present in us all, but when pronounced, the reality approach will not succeed. Another problem occurs when the client cannot accept the source of the authority. For a Christian counsellor, for example, this source must always be in scripture, which a non-Christian client may not accept as valid.

Non-directive counselling is the 'soft' approach. It emphasises the role of the person (not the counsellor) to recognise and then rectify his problems. The counsellor's role is to provide a non-judgemental setting in which it is possible for this to happen. The *premise* therefore is: the client must control and/or direct the content of the counselling sessions. Carl Rogers, who developed this approach, states that the way a person sees himself (self-concept) determines his behaviour. In fact, it is because the person has a distorted or untrue view of himself that he is emotionally sick. Rogerian therapy teaches that since a person acts out his view of himself, once this self-concept is corrected the behaviour will change in a constructive way too (Rogers, 1951). So the task of therapy is to transmit the client's current self-concept to him through the words of the counsellor. Rogers uses the example of a mirror to describe the counsellor. Even as a mirror gives back a picture of a person's physical appearance, so a counsellor should reflect back the client's psychological image (self-concept). This is done primarily by re-stating the emotional content in the client's words — a reflection of feelings. For example, as a client describes his reaction to being unemployed, the counsellor says, "You sound angry at yourself." This comment forces the client to "see" the source of the problem in his own unrecognised emotions which combine to form his self-concept. In this approach, the success of counselling depends upon the accuracy of the client's self-awareness.

The *procedure* used to promote this self-awareness in non-directive counselling is simply acceptance of the client. Each client must feel he is accepted unconditionally by the counsellor, that he is really valued for who he is rather than rejected for what he has done. When the counsellor knows him at his worst and still accepts him, this allows the client to accept himself — problems and all. Nothing the client does is ever condemned by the counsellor, as it is believed that only the client can and should judge his behaviour and that within the context of being loved and accepted by another.

However, this non-directive method often fails. It too is prohibited by certain circumstances. Whenever an individual has difficulty receiving love (unconditionally accepted) it is not appropriate. In cases of extreme guilt, to feel love only without condemnation makes the person feel more guilty. In an immature client, such as a retarded child or senile person, change will not occur simply because he feels accepted. Direction from another is essential in such cases, as self-direction is not possible.

In view of these inherent limitations in both the directive and non-directive approaches, the ideal would be to combine them. The more sensitive the counsellor is to the emotional state of the client, the more he will be able appropriately to apply each method. During the intense initial stages of counselling, the client may feel more comfortable if the content discussed is under his control (non-directive method). Later, as a relationship of trust in the counsellor has been established, confrontation and condemnation (directive method) might be best. But both approaches assume that the counsellor will be able to care genuinely about the client. Once this caring is communicated to the client, there is freedom to use either method. Personality variables, of both client and counsellor, are the guidelines here. Certainly this is where the discernment of the Holy Spirit is absolutely crucial for effective counselling.

Definite Goals of Counselling

How can we evaluate if a counselling method is effective? Goals are necessary for this evaluation. But without an agreement about these goals, there is no criterion for judging the consequences of counselling. There are three types (levels) of goals: the first is symptom relief; the second is behavioural change, and the third is self-insight. (See Figure 1 below)

Fig. 1 : *THE GOALS OF COUNSELLING*

> SYMPTOM RELIEF
> BEHAVIOURAL CHANGE
> SELF-INSIGHT

Psychological distress is painful. This means that most people seek counselling in order to obtain some symptom relief. They may suffer from insomnia, uncontrollable anger, debilitating fears, insatiable addictions, intense guilt, or marital arguments. They can no longer cope, find themselves trapped, and desperately want a way out of themselves. Although relief from immediate distress is sought, if it is given too soon the underlying problems will be ignored. Physically, it is like taking an aspirin to treat a headache; it deals with the pain (symptom) but not the problem (cause). Yet whenever psychic pain is intense, some relief must be given before any deeper problems may be handled. *Symptom relief* can be sudden, such as medication to allow sleep, or marital separation to avoid arguments. But there is a danger, if the reduction in distress is too dramatic, that the client's desire to solve the underlying issue may disappear. (If going home to mother is so satisfying, why bother to cope with the marital conflict!)

A deeper, and more difficult, goal of counselling is *behaviour change*, enabling the client to change his words, actions or reactions to stressful situations. A wife's nagging behaviour may change as she is helped to see how it triggers off many marital disputes. For behaviour change to take place the client must accept responsibility for the situation and change her own negative contribution to it. Within the counselling relationship the client experiences encouragement and/or confrontation of a kind that makes behavioural change possible.

The ultimate goal of counselling is *self-insight*. For a client to gain this self-insight it is necessary to probe deep into the unknown (unconscious) motives for his misery. This involves the pain of probing, but it achieves the goal of understanding the source of the problem. The client is encouraged to recall repressed feelings/memories and to accept a more accurate picture of the situation. A new understanding gives insight which releases the person from the bondage of the unknown. It may take time for the insights to be recognised and incorporated into the personality. But this is the process of inner healing. Months or years of counselling may be needed before a wife realises that the unconscious hatred of her father has been transferred to her husband and is now manifested in constant nagging. This insight brings the additional pain of guilt. Any competent counsellor should be able to develop such insights in the client, but in this case only the Christian counsellor can enable her to accept God's forgiveness of herself and then of that father too. Thus a spiritual perspective, based upon the supernatural experience of forgiveness, permits healing of an emotional experience.

Discerning the Client's Motives

Why does a client come for help? He may not be sure himself, but the motivation will be partly cognitive (having to do with thinking) and partly emotional (having to do with feeling). But the motive admitted by the client may not be the motive at work. Yet if the counsellor cannot discern the client's motives, he cannot help him either. These reasons for wanting counselling will contribute directly to the success or failure of the counselling relationship.

Common motives for beginning counselling are as follows:
1 to get attention;
2 to seek help and advice;
3 to confirm the client's self-righteousness, and
4 to give in to external pressure.

A client may enjoy the emphasis on himself that a sharing of problems will bring. He *gets attention*, his ego is built up as the counsellor demonstrates care for him, and, like a spoiled child, he will invent other problems to keep the attention coming. After all, if he were to improve his behaviour and act responsibly, he might lose this new source of caring. Thus his inner motive (to gain attention) keeps him from the healing that he says he is seeking. Confronted with this motive, the client may accept the insight offered and his genuine reason for continuing counselling.

The client who *seeks help and advice* is the easiest to counsel. He wants change, and knows he wants change and will face additional trauma to get it. He may be desperate, which makes it all the more important that he gets help from the right person. Perhaps he may try any advice given by anyone to alleviate some distress. The counsellor should be aware of this possibility and warn the client of the dangers of seeking help from multiple sources.

Among those who seek counselling in order to *confirm* their own self-righteousness, there are many Christians. Christian spouses may be 'delighted' to go to a Christian counsellor to confirm their righteousness in the marital conflict. If God and his moral laws condemn adultery, the offended partner may have his/her ego built up by an alliance with God! This self-righteousness is so blinding in its effect that the client cannot 'see' his/her own part in the problem. But in such a situation it is necessary for change in motivation to begin with the individual and then to extend to the situation as a whole. A confession of the sin of self-righteousness, and the resulting humility in the client, can do much to alter the whole situation constructively. If the self-righteousness remains unconfessed, the counselling produces stagnation only.

Another difficult motive to work with is found in the client who seeks counselling merely as a *response* to *external pressure*. In fact, his willingness to co-operate in counselling goes no further than an agreement to turn up for an appointment. He is externally giving in to the pressure of a parent, spouse, child, minister, employer, etc, who believes the client needs help. But beneath the apparent acquiescence in coming there may be defiance and daring, defiance in not submitting to the need to change himself and daring in challenging the counsellor to make him change against his will. A teenager brought by a Christian parent, or a senile older person pushed to seek counselling by his frustrated child, are examples of such a client. In such a situation it is essential to win the respect of the client by reminding him that only he can change the situation — if he wants to. The non-directive approach may also encourage the client who lacks self-respect because he is passive in the situation, to develop more healthy motives.

The counsellor must discern the client's motives. But he must also confront the client with them. This is because all but the second category are counter-productive in counselling. They hinder the healing process, and their negative influence must be pointed out to the client. Exactly when and how this confrontation is to occur depends upon the discernment of the Holy Spirit again. But to proceed in counselling without this confrontation is to ensure continued distress for both client and counsellor alike.

Description of a Christian Counsellor

The New Testament contains various descriptions of the qualities needed by Christian leaders. Even though there is no church office labelled 'counsellor', many of the characteristics given for elders and deacons would apply to counsellors too. The list of requirements for an elder given in 1 Timothy 3:2-7 includes: being —

"above reproach, the husband of but one wife, temperate, self-controlled, respectable, hospitable, able to teach, not given to much wine, not violent but gentle, not quarrelsome, not a lover of money. He must manage his own family well and see that his children obey him with proper respect. (If anyone does not know how to manage his own family, how can he take care of God's church?) He must not be a recent convert, or he may become conceited and fall under the same judgement as the devil. He must also have a good reputation with outsiders, so that he will not fall into disgrace and into the devil's trap."

These verses identify three qualities which are necessary in a counsellor: maturity, meekness, and mastery. Maturity is essential in a chronological sense, so that the person will have lived long enough himself to have experienced rejections, hurts, misunderstandings, moodiness, etc, from others. A competent teenage counsellor is rare, yet an eighty-year-old may be insensitive to emotional realities. Thus, age in itself may not be significant, but it is important to have some direct experience of the depths of anxiety. It seems that the most sensitive counsellors are those who have either personally gone through emotional traumas or who have stood alongside a family member in their particular agony. This kind of direct exposure produces a maturity that transcends years alone. Besides emotional maturity, spiritual maturity is also important: a recent convert is not the ideal Christian counsellor. Spiritual and emotional growth constantly interact with each other — but there should be evidence of both. If there is growth in both areas then there is an inner peace which allows the person to cope under crisis. Others may become hysterical or withdraw, but the mature person (psychologically and spiritually) will gain respect by stepping securely into the crisis situation. Doing so may be an act of faith, as he will not know what to do or say beforehand, but his trust is in the Lord who will give wisdom to act precisely when it is needed. This assurance of God's presence supplies an inner security in times of crisis.

The second major characteristic of a Christian counsellor is meekness. The 1 Timothy passage speaks of being gentle, not violent nor quarrelsome, yet able to teach (counsel). A counsellor must relate well to people, to know how to express warmth and concern, and when to keep quiet and just listen. He must genuinely like people, and his gentleness must include a quality of strength that makes empathy possible. Empathy is literally the ability to feel with the client, metaphorically to crawl out of your own skin and enter the skin or experience of the other person. It is good if the counsellor has himself experienced various types of distress, but the ability to empathise is closely related to the counsellor's inherent meekness. If he is so full of himself and arrogant, how can he let go of self long enough to enter into the suffering of another? If he cannot empathise he cannot communicate understanding to the client. Another aspect of meekness is to be available to the client, to be "there", or even to open up his home (hospitableness). Being available is difficult. For to be totally available for ministry on a twenty-four hour a day basis leads to frustrations for the individual and his/her family. Maturity from a balanced life is the only answer: to be totally available for clients within a reasonable time period and then to develop other involvements too. It takes meekness to maintain a counselling relationship and still realise that as a counsellor you are not and should never become the only source of the client's strength.

Mastery is the third essential characteristic of the effective counsellor. Self-control or mastery appear in the 1 Timothy passage as the ability to maintain a marriage/personal relationship, manage one's own home and children, regulate physical desires such as that for wine, control economic pressures to acquire more money, and to be aware of the "devil's trap" of becoming conceited. The word temperate summarises these areas of control — not given to extremes, either from within (emotional moodiness), or from without (cultural conformity). Thus, self-mastery gives discipline to the Christian life from which the delights of a mature personality may emerge.

Selection procedures based on these biblical criteria should be used by any Christian counselling service. It is obvious that only a few are qualified in these terms. Although many will thus be excluded, it is far better to train and work with those who are mature. Another factor to remember: maturity means interdependence not independence. Therefore, even the most mature person will need support from fellow-counsellors, both in his own personal situation and in relating to his clients. If any potential counsellor protests that he can minister best alone, the power of conceit is at work. Sharing of oneself in a mutual way demonstrates Christ's love within the body of believers. But it is

Chapter Three
Spiritual Preparation of the Counsellor

COUNSELLING is dangerous work. The psyche of the client is exposed in varying degrees to the discerning mind of the counsellor. But what if the counsellor is unable to discern, and in fact contributes to the distortion of the problem? This possibility is real, especially when the counsellor is poorly prepared for the work. But the preparation involves more than just knowledge of the counselling process and client — it requires training in the spiritual realm as well. To state the obvious first, the counsellor must be a committed Christian. This means he must be aware of the realities of sin and forgiveness, God's judgement and love, man's emptiness within and fulfilment in Christ (2 Corinthians 5:16-21). Each of these basic spiritual truths must be applied in experience. The counsellor will have been convicted of sin (Romans 3:23), have turned toward Christ who paid the penalty for that sin (Romans 5:8-11) and then by faith accepted the grace of God. This action restores the person to a relationship with God as Father (who seeks), Son (who saves) and Holy Spirit (who sanctifies).

As a result of this commitment, a spiritual transaction or covenant is made between God and the individual (Jeremiah 31:33-34; Ephesians 2:12-22). Because of it the Christian now possesses eternal life (1 John 5:13), and the proof of this new life is a supernatural ability to love others (John 13:34-35). Once the fear of death has been conquered in the cross of Christ, the individual is free to become all he is capable of being via the Holy Spirit (Galatians 5:13-26). No individual can live the Christian life without falling desperately into sin and selfishness each day, but he can choose to submit to Christ (Romans 12:1-2), and as "a result he does not live the rest of his earthly life for evil human desires, but rather for the will of God" (1 Peter 4:2). In this covenant relationship, the Christian is daily conformed in basic character into the very likeness of Christ his Lord (Romans

8:29). This character or personality transformation affects in time all areas of thinking, willing and feeling (Romans 12:1-2). This is maturity for a Christian, and it is this type of spiritual maturity which is essential in the ministry of counselling. Certain spiritual attitudes will be the outward signs of this inner state of growth. Some of these necessary attitudes are described in this chapter; as such they become barometers to measure the quality of spiritual preparation for counselling.

A Clear Conscience — 1 Peter 3:15-16

"But in your heart set apart Christ as Lord. Always be prepared to give an answer to everyone who asks you to give the reason for the hope that you have. But do this with gentleness and respect, keeping a clear conscience, so that those who speak maliciously against your good behaviour in Christ may be ashamed of their slander."

An effective Christian counsellor must have a clear channel toward God. In both thought and behaviour, Christ must be in charge — to be set apart as Lord. If the opposite is true for the counsellor, the 'self' becomes lord and as a consequence motives can be distorted (will), feelings can be over-sensitive (emotion), and ideas can be rationalisations (intellect). In essence the goal of counselling then becomes a glorification of the counsellor. But when Christ is indeed Lord of the total person, the distractions of selfishness are soon perceived as sin and then confessed to God first and if necessary to man second. This maintains the direct fellowship with God, from which discernment for counselling must come.

Fellowship with God is crucial. It is the role of the conscience to censor anything that threatens this relationship to God. It is through the conscience that any sin must be first acknowledged and then confessed in spirit and corrected in behaviour. Only when this cleansing process continues daily is the person able to maintain spiritual communication with God. With the corrective of a clear conscience, the individual Christian is able to perceive the problems in others because he has first perceived the sin in self. Thus the discernment of the Holy Spirit has a direct channel to work through, and in humility the counsellor communicates gentleness and respect to the client. Any sin, especially the sin of self-righteousness, will disrupt this twofold communication process — vertically with God and horizontally with man. Humility is the hallmark of a clear conscience (from a human perspective); and discernment is the distinction of a cleansed conscience (from a divine perspective). Both characteristics are crucial prerequisites for any individual Christian to be prepared to counsel. Both characteristics are the consequence of a conscience daily made sensitive to the convictions of the Holy Spirit.

Be Prepared to Listen — James 1:19

"My dear brothers, take note of this: everyone should be quick to listen, slow to speak and slow to become angry."

Listening involves learning; learning necessitates listening. In counselling the two processes overlap continually, so that an effective counsellor must listen. The counsellor should be "quick to listen", as the first (almost automatic) focus is on what the client is saying and how it is being said. To do this the counsellor cannot concentrate on what his response to the client's comments should be. Most people are poor listeners because rather than really thinking about what is being said by the other person, they mentally rehearse an appropriate response in advance. In this way, they are quick to speak and slow to listen, in the exact opposite of the scriptural injunction! Perhaps it is fear that motivates this preparation in thought, fear of saying the "wrong" thing to the client. But this fear is futile, since there must be a reliance anyway upon the Holy Spirit within to provide a relevant response. A concentration on the client, really listening, makes the counsellor's feelings secondary. Then any emotional reaction by the counsellor, be it in sympathy or in anger is much less likely to prejudge the problem before the facts are revealed by the client. Intense listening enables the counsellor to remain emotionally neutral toward the problem and at the same time emotionally positive toward the person. The client realises the priorities at work in the counsellor and senses that he is important enough to be genuinely listened to as a person.

Also, in a spiritual sense, the discipline of listening is part of the general personality trait of self-control. "If anyone is never at fault in what he says, he is a perfect man, able to keep his whole body in check" (James 3:2b). A mind controlled by the

Holy Spirit is always ready to listen, to focus out extraneous material and to discern what it is essential to know about a particular person. It means a concentration on the 'now', to pick up accurately the many nuances of meaning being communicated; it is not a reaching back into past history, nor is it leaping forward into future happenings. But as more of the meaning of the 'now' is perceived, the proper focus of the past and future is ensured for the client as a whole. Listening done in this way is work! But if the inability so to listen is confessed to the Lord, strength plus ability is supernaturally given to the Christian counsellor for the task.

Be a Burden-bearer — Galatians 6:1-3

"Brothers, if someone is caught in a sin, you who are spiritual should restore him gently. But watch yourself, or you also may be tempted. Carry each other's burdens, and in this way you will fulfil the law of Christ. If anyone thinks he is something when he is nothing, he deceives himself."

A client's burden must be borne by someone other than himself. A person can become trapped by the power of his own problems. But another brother or sister who is in a right spiritual relationship to God can release the person. In order to achieve this, the counsellor must have the right 'spiritual attitude'. This attitude is revealed in three ways: (1) how the restoration is made; (2) what the motive for the restoration/counselling really is; and (3) what the consequence of the restoration turns out to be for the counsellor.

A client overwhelmed by a burden must be restored by the counsellor via one method — gentleness. To restore means to put something back in its rightful place, symbolically to set a broken limb so that it can be healed properly from within. This is an accurate picture of the counselling process, to put emotional distress back into a healthy context (one of balance) from which healing may emerge. But if this is done too abruptly, then like the broken limb, the force applied can shatter rather than restore. When a counsellor is gentle, he is acting out of respect for the sensitivities of the person and the seriousness of the problem. The strength of gentleness, not the strength of agressiveness is needed by the counsellor because of the complexities of emotional situations. And the source of that strength for the Christian counsellor is always the Holy Spirit (Galatians 5:22).

The Galatians passage gives the 'correct' spiritual motive for counselling. It is a willingness to carry another's burden because of obedience to Christ. By implication, it is also a willingness to let go of another's burden when necessary. There will always be many people needing psychological help, but will the Christian counsellor respond in love or out of duty? It depends upon whom the counsellor responds to first. If his heart is in daily submission to Christ, then it is possible to have a non-possessive love for the client. But if his motive is to please a demanding client, then it degenerates into counselling from a sense of duty. A counsellor may be trapped by the desire to please the client rather than Christ. Obedience to Christ, as a motive in the counsellor, keeps priorities in their proper perspective. This obedience produces inevitable consequences for the Christian counsellor. An awareness of one's own weaknesses will be part of the "watching or you also may be tempted". This awareness will not permit the client to be seen as an inferior being who has yielded to spiritual/emotional/physical pressures to sin. Rather the client is viewed as an equal to the counsellor, equal in vulnerability to stress. This keeps the counsellor aware of his own limitations. And these limitations will not allow the counsellor to believe that his skill is really the most important aspect in counselling. If counselling another convicts the counsellor of his own weaknesses and sins — then there is a release of God's healing power in that counsellor.

Be Willing to Show Love — Galatians 5:13

"You, my brothers, were called to be free. But do not use your freedom to indulge the sinful nature; rather serve one another in love."

A Christian is a servant. Paradoxically, it is only because the Christian is being freed from himself, that a genuine serving of another is possible. Selfishness, a consideration of the self first, leaves no possibility of being a servant of others. The client must always come first — only after a submission to the Lord. When this is not so, the Christian becomes angry every time he is expected to serve the client — whether in accepting a changing of the time of the appointment or in giving advice without apparent acceptance. This anger becomes an attitude of resentment in the counsellor, because his needs are being violated by the demands of the client; at this point selfishness is sovereign. Counselling with this attitude makes it a burden not a ministry unto the Lord. The problem is that the counsellor has not been broken enough before the Lord to become a willing servant of others.

Spiritual and/or emotional immaturity encourages this attitude of selfishness. A group of immature fellow Christians may distort counselling into a type of 'ego fulfilment' or an individual Christian can become just too proud, too busy or even too spiritual to be an effective counsellor. When this happens the counsellor is not willing to be hurt (misunderstood) by the client, nor 'contaminated' by his moral behaviour. Any counsellor who believes he is superior to the client cannot be a servant. But the Lord gives the counsellor the ability to serve the client. As the client's needs are served, so is the Lord.

Be Empathetic — 2 Corinthians 1:3-5

"Praise be to the God and Father of our Lord Jesus Christ, the Father of compassion and God of all comfort, who comforts us in all our troubles, so that we can comfort those in any trouble with the comfort we ourselves have received from God. For just as the sufferings of Christ flow over into our lives, so also through Christ our comfort overflows."

The scriptural principle for counselling is this: the amount given depends on the amount received. Because the counsellor is being comforted in his own problems by God, he is able to be of comfort to others. In this way the counsellor becomes a channel for communicating compassion from God to the client — but in the meanwhile his own emotional hurts are healed too! First God himself becomes the counsellor to the Christian, who then is able to be a counsellor to the client.

When the Christian is aware of his troubles, they may be brought before God, and this process begins. But the Christian counsellor can deceive himself. He can minimise and/or deny the difficulties so that they are never acknowledged to self or God. Repressed hurts are not healed in the Christian, they just become deeper hurts. This will block communication with the client. But when those hurts are exposed to the love of God, emotional healing is experienced within the counsellor. As the counsellor is being made whole, he is spiritually prepared to counsel.

This preparation includes the counsellor's learning of empathy. Without empathy there is no effective counselling. Empathy is being able to put oneself into the position of another, to feel as that person feels in a particular situation. Essentially it is an identification with the client's hurts, so they are also felt by the counsellor. It is easier for the counsellor to enter into the experience of another if he has had a similar experience himself. Then the strength of Christ is shared from those experiences of his own which are similar to the client's. Either an unmet need or an unknown experience in the counsellor will prevent the development of empathy. To try to help a client with a problem, when a similar problem in the counsellor has not been helped — this is hypocrisy. But to encourage the client to apply principles for growth, principles proven valid in the counsellor's life — this is true spirituality.

This spirituality comes from a dynamic relationship with the "God of all comfort". The Lord comforts the counsellor by giving the strength to struggle through to emotional victories and the sufferings to allow empathy to develop. Strength and sufferings have the same purpose, each makes the Christian more like the Lord. The counsellor who abides in Christ receives both strength (to understand) and suffering (to empathise) so that he may learn to serve the client. Why? Because the Christian has a Sovereign Counsellor. This assurance prepares the Christian spiritually for a counselling ministry.

Counselling and Demonic Influences

Basic Principles

Clients come with complex problems. Could any of these be caused by Satanic influences? The mind of the counsellor is moulded by many factors. Could any of these be caused by demonic influences? A Christian counsellor should face these possibilities within the client and within himself. But this is both a difficult and a dangerous area to investigate.

Two extremes in thinking produce the difficulty. The first,

coming from a super-spiritual Christianity, labels *all* emotional problems as demonic in nature; while the second, being the product of scientific sophistication, denies that anything demonic could exist in our modern world. However, the truth is that both extremes are wrong. The Christian counsellor must avoid both of these errors by neither always expecting nor always denying the demonic. Each client must be evaluated individually, to determine when demonic forces are at work and when they are not. Above all, the counsellor must be aware of demonic influences upon his own thinking/attitudes.

It is also dangerous to analyze the demonic. There is a warning not to learn "Satan's so-called deep secrets" (Rev. 2:24). Yet the Christian must still be alert because the "enemy the devil prowls around like a roaring lion looking for someone to devour" (I Peter 5:8). The Christian counsellor is especially vulnerable, for his time, strength and effectiveness can each be 'devoured' by a particular client. Without discernment regarding the demonic at work in such a client, these subtle attacks can summate over time to destroy a counselling ministry. With discernment of the demonic, the real problem is exposed and the counsellor may then use the weapons of spiritual warfare. The counsellor must continually put on the full armour of God in order to "stand against the devil's schemes" (Eph. 6:11).

Satan uses many methods or schemes to apply one basic principle. It is this: the greater the degree of obedience to Christ the greater the amount of opposition from Satan. A disobedient (ineffective) Christian need not be stopped, and thus may never experience direct demonic attacks. Christian counselling is part of a general healing ministry in the Church. Therefore, any Christian who is obedient to a call of God to serve in this capacity will certainly be exposed to the subtle schemes of Satan. And as his ministry grows so will the intensity of these attacks.

Satanic Methods

Satan's methods are legion. But the attacks usually fall into one of the following categories: (1) distrust; (2) distraction; or (3) disguise. The devil is first shown in scripture as a being who creates doubt (distrust) about some aspect of God. Thus Eve is encouraged to doubt God's word when the Serpent asks, "Did God really say . . .?" (Gen. 3:1). In a similar way, a Christian counsellor may be tempted to distrust God's power to heal a particular client, his own calling to a counselling ministry, or even the necessity for counselling within the church. As these doubts grow, discouragement is produced which could slowly but surely destroy a ministry of caring for the emotional needs of others. This destruction may come directly from the demonic influences upon the thinking of the counsellor.

Another effective method is distraction. The essence of Satan's temptation of Christ was to get Him to take the good and give up the best. Christ was encouraged to satisfy normal physical needs for food, to misuse psychological needs for power and to bypass the Cross and take His spiritual right to rule now (Matt. 4:1-11). Likewise a Christian counsellor may have his own priorities tested by Satan. Will he think first of his own monetary (physical) needs and second of the emotional hurts of the client? Will the counsellor be tempted to go on an ego trip, where psychological skill must be 'proven' by helping a particular client? Or will he be distracted to bypass the long (often painful) process of probing into the roots of the client's problem and just deal with surface symptoms? In many such ways, the counsellor may be effectively distracted by the devil from concentrating on the best method or the real source of the client's hurts.

Disguise is a favourite demonic method. Satan is pictured in scripture masquerading as an "angel of light" (2 Cor. 11:13-14), and speaking as the father of lies (John 8:44). Satan disguises evil as good and good as evil. For example, a male counsellor may be tempted to believe that if he encourages the seductive behaviour of a female client, he will be helping her to become healthier by 'expressing feelings'. An extension of this same 'lie' would condone adultery as a necessary antidote for a sick marriage. Another form of disguise is to convince the counsellor that a specific method of counselling or a prominent counsellor has all the answers. By implication scriptural truths are irrelevant. More and more time is therefore given to learning the 'good' secular methods to the neglect of scriptural study. This lie may also be shown in the reverse. Then the counsellor is tempted to apply *only* scriptural verses in counselling and to denounce as demonic any valid psychological insight or method. All truth comes from God, and can never contradict the Scripture unless one or the other is distorted. But if Satan has been successful in creating confusion in the mind of the counsellor, then the counsellor is not prepared to counsel.

Christian Counter Attacks

How can the Christian counsellor learn to conquer these demonic influences? Recognition of Satan's methods is the essential first step, but an application of the principles of spiritual warfare must follow. Satan attacks but he can be defeated. "The accuser of our brothers, who accuses them before our God day and night, has been hurled down. They overcame him by the blood of the Lamb, and by the word of their testimony; they did not love their lives so much as to shrink from death. Therefore rejoice, you heavens and you who dwell in them! But woe to the earth and the sea, because the devil has gone down to you! He is filled with fury, because he knows that his time is short" (Rev. 12:10-12)

The Christian must indeed deal with a furious adversary. But victory is always available in the cross of Christ. Spiritual battles require spiritual resources. Specifically, these methods for counteracting demonic influences include: discipline, discernment and direct action.

More important than anything else, the Christian counsellor must be disciplined. This means an inner consistency in his spirit nature as he continues to love Christ more than his own life (Rev. 12:11). Regular times of prayer, scripture reading and fellowship with other Christians will help maintain this healthy spiritual perspective. Impure motives (double mindedness) toward clients, extremes in the application of counselling methods, critical attitudes toward fellow counsellors, or a general discouragement about counselling — all provide open doors for demonic activity. But in each of these examples, a daily submission of self to God will produce victory over the devil (James 4:7-8). Satan exploits any extreme in attitude or behaviour; but discipline prevents extremes. In this way, a spiritually disciplined life becomes a healthy (balanced) personality.

A self-controlled or disciplined counsellor is alerted to Satan's activities (I Peter 5:8), and then is able to pray effectively about them (I Peter 4:7). This is an application of the gift of discernment. Discipline provides the foundation for a counter attack toward Satan; and discernment provides the basis for both prayer and action. To see satanic influences when they are present and not to see them when they are absent — this is supernatural discernment. With this discernment, the cause of the problem is exposed and then the counsellor has the responsibility to act appropriately.

Direct action against the demonic takes many forms. A prayer for the protection of the counsellor, claiming the blood of Christ to cover his whole being is the first course of action. Persevering prayer with another Christian is always best. By uniting together victory over the demonic can be claimed for a specific client, or for the clarification of the counsellor's confused thinking during a time of temptation. Exorcism, when there is direct evidence of demon possession in a client, should only be done by someone experienced in this type of ministry. Prayer will confirm the presence of the demonic, the cross of Christ will conquer the demonic, and the counsellor is then spiritually prepared to counsel.

Points for Discussion

1 Why may counselling be considered 'dangerous' for the client? How may a spiritually prepared counsellor minimise this danger? *psyche exposed*

2 What does it mean to be a committed Christian? What are the basic beliefs and essential behaviours that characterise the Christian?

3 How may a Christian maintain a clear conscience? What will be the consequences, especially in a counselling ministry, if he/she does not?

4 Why is listening so difficult? How may the counsellor's listening ability be improved?

5 How does the Scripture say burdens should be shared within the Christian community? What are the dangers of bearing someone's burdens in the wrong way or for the wrong reasons?

6 How must a Christian counsellor be like a servant — in attitude and behaviour?

7   Why must each counsellor have a counsellor? What happens if the Christian counsellor is not allowing the Lord to be his/her Counsellor? What happens when the Lord does counsel the counsellor — how does this increase counselling effectiveness?

8   What is empathy? Why is it necessary in counselling? How may a Christian counsellor be better able to develop an attitude of empathy?

9   Why is it both necessary yet difficult to deal with demonic influences in counselling?

10 What are some of the specific methods Satan uses to stop a counsellor who is responding obediently to Christ?

11 How may a Christian counsellor effectively recognize and overcome demonic influences in his ministry?

distrust
distrest
disguise

Discipline
Discern
Direct action

PART II
Development of Perspectives for Counselling

CHAPTER FOUR
A Christian View of Personality

WHAT is normality? What is abnormal behaviour? Since most people, including psychologists, vehemently disagree as to what is normal, criteria or "norms" are needed to describe human nature. For the Christian, these norms must describe man's personality as it is presented in Scripture. In the perspective of God's truth, man's personality may then be considered 'normal' or 'abnormal'.

The Created Form for the Person: Body, Mind, Spirit

The Bible does give a pattern of personality functioning (normality) and/or malfunctioning (abnormality). Several passages describe man's nature in the ideal, as the created image of God himself (Psalm 8). The best summary of an individual personality is found in 1 Thessalonians 5:23, "May your whole spirit, soul and body be kept blameless at the coming of our Lord Jesus Christ." Here a three-fold aspect of personality is presented: the body (soma), the mind/soul (psyche), and the spirit (pneuma). See Figure 2 overleaf.

A *body* is the most obvious part of the person. The primary purpose of the body is to communicate with the physical world through the senses. Seeing, hearing, touching, etc, are all functions of the body. All functions of the body can be traced back to conception when the fertilised egg divides into three layers of cells — called the Ectoderm, Mesoderm, and Endoderm. A division of cells continues as the Ectoderm develops into brain and nerve tissue; the Mesoderm becomes muscle tissue and bone, and the Endoderm evolves into the organs of digestion. The completed physical structure (body), enables the person to relate to other physical things — the lights, sounds, tastes, smells, touches, etc, of the environment. How accurate (or inaccurate) this communication of physical stimuli to the brain

Fig. 2 : **THE CREATED FORM OF THE PERSON** (*1 THESSALONIANS 5 : 23*)

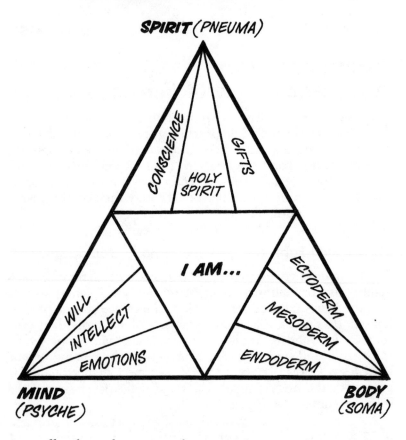

SPIRIT *(PNEUMA)*

CONSCIENCE

GIFTS

HOLY SPIRIT

I AM...

WILL

INTELLECT

EMOTIONS

ECTODERM

MESODERM

ENDODERM

MIND *(PSYCHE)*   **BODY** *(SOMA)*

is, will often determine the normality or abnormality of behaviour.

A second part of the person is the *mind*. The primary purpose of the mind is to communicate with itself and others. It can be called 'personality' or 'mind', and it is the unique pattern of human qualities that makes each person different. It also has three accepted sub-divisions: the will, the intellect, and the emotions. Specialisation in function occurs. The will's purpose is to choose, in biblical language to lust after things (1 John 2:16); the intellect's is to think, biblically to reason along with God (Isaiah 1:18); whilst the emotions are meant to feel, being symbolised in Scripture as the heart of man (Mark 7:21). Inter-actions among these three aspects of the mind/psyche are constant, but such communication may be healthy or diseased.

The third part of the person is the *spirit*. History gives evidence of a basic spiritual need in man to relate to eternal values and to God himself. Thus, all societies, from the stone age to modern eras, show man in the act of worship. Neither bread (to satisfy a bodily need), nor logic (to satisfy a mental need), will be able to satisfy the spirit of man. The spirit nature allows the person to transcend his physical and psychological environment to seek communication with God. Its three suggested parts are: the conscience; the Holy Spirit (in a born-again Christian); and the gifts (talents). Spiritual functions differ with each part. The conscience is the moral agent in man, internalising the principles of right and wrong according to each culture. The person is partly aware of the censorship of the conscience, while the rest of the conscience operates on an unconscious level. There is a vacuum, a 'dead area' in the spiritual nature of each person, which can be made alive only by the entrance of the Holy Spirit at conversion (Romans 6:13, 8:6, 1 Corinthians 2:12). The non-Christian's personality is thus incomplete; many spiritual realities are beyond his awareness. But in the Christian, the whole spirit nature becomes alive and functions by interpreting spiritual realities to the person. The spirit dimension also includes gifts. A biblical list of such gifts would include prophesying, teaching, administration, service, wisdom, faith, healing, tongues (Romans 12:6-8, 1 Corinthians 12:7-11, 1 Peter 4:8-11). These spiritual 'talents' are potentially in each person, and some non-Christians may develop one or more in particular. But it is only the Christian, whose spirit nature is alive to God, who can perfect his potential abilities for the good of all.

The Co-ordinated Form Leading to Wholeness

The three aspects of the person, body, mind and spirit, are to be kept in wholeness or health until Christ comes again (1 Thessalonians 5:23). Such soundness can be the result only of health in each part and the co-ordination among the parts (see Figure 2). The spirit nature is meant to regulate and maintain the healthy balance within the other two parts (Romans 8:9-11).

Because of the indwelling Spirit of God (1 Corinthians

6:19-20), both the mind and the body may be kept in balance. For the Christian, a wonderful privilege exists for his mind. It need not remain in a state of confusion, with a stubborn will (Isaiah 48:4), futile thinking (Romans 1:21) and impure motives (James 4:8-10). Rather the Christian is told that he has taken off his "old self with its practices and has put on the new self, which is being renewed in knowledge in the image of its creator" (Colossians 3:10). This renewal of the mind (Romans 12:2) is possible as the will of the person chooses to submit his body *and* mind to the perfect will of God. It is this act of submission to God that releases the power of the Holy Spirit to renew the mind, and through the mind to maintain health in the whole personality. The primary source of knowledge needed to achieve this wholeness comes from the Scripture which is "living and active. Sharper than any double-edged sword, it penetrates even to dividing soul and spirit, joints and marrow: it judges the thoughts and attitudes of the heart" (Hebrews 4:12).

This verse tells how important the word of God is in maintaining balance in the personality. It also shows how strong the natural connections are among the three parts of the person. These co-ordinations mean that whatever occurs in one part will affect the other two parts. For example, fasting is a physical act (body) which produces clearer thinking (mind) and new power in prayer (spirit). Repressed anger (mind) may produce hypertension (body) and difficulty in prayer (spirit). For this very reason Peter exhorts the Christian to "be clear minded and self-controlled so that you can pray" (1 Peter 4:7).

The Confused Form Leading to Psychological Imbalance

Since the Holy Spirit maintains wholeness in the personality, it may seem as if the Christian has his mental health assured. But many Christians do have acute emotional distress. It must therefore be possible for something to go wrong within their personalities. If a distortion/disease occurs in any one part (body, mind, spirit), sickness is produced within the whole. Thus, the type of interactions among the three parts can create either balance or imbalance. Knowledge is needed to realise how to renew the mind (Colossians 3:10), as well as how to understand the Christian who is emotionally sick.

Distortions within the Person

As there are three interrelated parts to the person, so there are three possible sources of sickness within that individual. Either the body, or the mind, or the spirit may be distorted which will develop into some form of sickness. See Figure 3.

BODY		DISEASE (GENETICS), DIET
MIND	WILL INTELLECT EMOTIONS	ADDICTIONS, COMPULSIONS DELUSIONS, PARANOIA PHOBIAS, ANXIETY
SPIRIT		DISOBEDIENCE, DEMONS

Fig. 3 : **THE SOURCES OF DISORDER WITHIN THE PERSON**

A psychological disorder, whether in a Christian or non-Christian, may have its source in the body. Many of the more serious mental illnesses have their origin in the genetic make-up of the person. That misunderstood disease, schizophrenia, has been shown to have a strong genetic input, so do most of the other forms of psychoses. Some types of mental retardation are likewise genetic, e.g. mongoloidism. There are examples of diseases begun before the person is born, through a unique combination of genes from parents, grandparents and great-grandparents, etc. Other psychological diseases develop later and may slow down the circulation to the brain (senility), upset the proper balance of hormones (post-partum depression), or speed up the functioning of the nervous system (hyperkenesis). With a hyperkenetic, or hyperactive, child, the psychological symptoms seem to be stimulated via another physical factor — diet. Research has shown that the less sugar consumed by such a child, the more control he has over his behaviour.

A malfunctioning of the mind may be the source of many psychological problems. The lusts of an uncontrollable *will* produce addictions of both the mind and body (alcoholism). An *intellect* may develop a thinking pattern of delusions or paranoia. Delusions are false beliefs that are accepted as valid. They are a type of self-deception, whereby the behaviour becomes more and more difficult to understand rationally. For example, why would a beautiful, intelligent twenty-year-old girl choose as boyfriends only those who are violent towards her? The delusion at work here is "I am worthless and unlovable". As long as this 'belief' remains, no real progress can be made in counselling. Even the counsellor may be deliberately or unconsciously alienated to provoke his rejection of her and thus further "prove" her worthlessness.

Paranoia is a basic inability to trust others. This leads to a heightened sense of suspicion, which makes impossible most supportive relationships with other people. Thus the paranoid begins by thinking others are out to hurt him and ends by being unable to trust and therefore love anyone, including himself. This symptom is particularly disturbing for it erodes the effectiveness of the treatment most needed — a supportive counselling relationship.

The *emotional* component of the mind is also likely to be the source of mental illness. Fears become irrational and are labelled phobias, anger may be repressed and produces colitis (a psychosomatic disease), jealousy leads to possessive behaviour which destroys the other person, or hate may turn to bitterness which develops into a depression. Any particular emotion can get out of balance to produce mental illness.

The spirit nature of man is the third possible source of psychological problems. Disobedience and demonic activity both work through this spirit dimension to produce imbalance in the total person. Whenever God reveals something of his will and the Christian refuses to heed it, a state of disobedience occurs. The symptoms may be insomnia in the body and anger in the psyche, but the source is still disobedience. In this case, neither sleeping medication, nor a supportive non-directive counselling relationship, can heal the person. Only obedience to God will produce healing here. It is up to the Christian counsellor to discern the source of distress and then confront the client (when appropriate) with his specific disobedience. More difficult to understand is the power of Satan to control and/or confuse the activities of man. Demonic power is immense. Satan may accuse the Christian regarding past sins which were long forgiven (Revelation 12:10), mislead the Christian regarding present insights (Matthew 16:22), torment the Christian regarding his faith in God (Luke 22:31), and afflict the Christian with specific suffering (2 Corinthians 12:7). Yet in each case, the power of Satan is within the limits prescribed by the sovereignty of God (Job 1:12). Another source of irrational behaviour both in biblical times (Mark 5:2-16) and in our own is demon possession. Exorcism by those in the Church prepared for such a ministry is essential here. But each Christian counsellor must be aware that demonic oppression or possession is always a possible source of mental illness.

Each of these causes of psychological chaos, coming from the body, mind or spirit of the person, must be known to the Christian counsellor. Ignorance can produce costly mistakes. If the cause is misinterpreted, the counselling approach will be inappropriate. Thus it is just as disastrous to assume demonic involvement when there is none, as it is dangerous not to recognise demonic activity when it does exist. In either case the treatment will be wrong. The method of treatment in counselling is *always* related to the assumed cause; this makes it essential for the counsellor to know the 'right' cause. Supernatural discernment, given especially during times of prayer for the client, is needed. Personal consultation with more experienced counsellors and/or medical doctors, is needed too. Above all, the counsellor's psychological insights grow as he deliberately disciplines his mind to learn and his spirit to discern. Only the Christian counsellor can possess the power of knowledge, plus the discernment of the Holy Spirit, to recognise the source of disease. A medical doctor is trained to see sickness in the body, a psychiatrist to view problems as coming from the mind, and a minister to detect sin as the source of sickness in the spirit. But the Christian counsellor can develop a perspective which takes in all the possible sources of illness. The client is then evaluated through the created form of body, mind and spirit.

Description of the Basic Needs of the Person

There is a lot of ignorance about the basic needs of the body, mind and spirit. But if any need is unrealised, it creates tension — the frustration of unrealised potential. This frustration can produce imbalance in the personality. An unmet need can develop disease just as much as the active processes outlined previously. Therefore the Christian counsellor must both know and encourage his clients to fulfil these needs for wholeness of the person. See Figure 4 below.

BODY	MIND	SPIRIT
APPETITES ACTIVITY	ACCEPTANCE ACCOMPLISHMENT	WORSHIP WARFARE WITNESS

Fig. 4: **THE BASIC NEEDS OF THE PERSON**

Bodily needs if unmet produce strong states of motivation. Physical pain, hunger, thirst and sex are among the strongest of all motives. This is because the body is meant to be respected, in the Christian sense accepted as a gift from God. The physical creation (the body) reflects the wisdom of the Creator, so all the intricate bodily processes proclaim the wisdom of God. According to 1 Corinthians 6:19, the body may also become the temple of the Holy Spirit. So a good question to ask a Christian client is, "How are you taking care of God's property?"

Proper care involves the awareness and fulfilment of needs. For the body, the basic needs are: appetites and activity. The *appetites* include the normal desires for food, sleep, clothing, and sex. To satisfy these desires, neither too much nor too little of the object is needed. Thus over-eating (the biblical term is gluttony) is just as unhealthy as starvation. Too much sleeping can indicate a withdrawal pattern, even as insomnia indicates an anxiety state. Sex can become an obsession, which is abnormal, or it can be repressed into non-existence, which is equally unhealthy. Moderation is the norm, as regulated by the age and general health of the person.

Activity is the second physical need. It means two things: exercise and change. Deep within the physiology of the body is a need for movement; some animals, like hamsters, take their pleasure via an activity wheel. Conversely, there is a special kind of frustration that comes from non-movement. Any bed-ridden patient will agree to that. But with exercise there is an automatic release of tension, so that even fatigue can feel fantastic. Boredom is one of the major miseries of man. It can be overcome only by change. Some variation in routine, location, food and people stimulates health. Persons differ widely here; the more extroverted the personality, the greater this need for change. But some degree of change is essential for the functioning of a healthy body. Pehaps this is why the Lord gave the regulations regarding a sabbath of rest. He knew that such a renewal met a physical need.

The needs of the psyche (mind) must be met also or imbalance will occur. These basic psychological needs are: acceptance and accomplishment. *Acceptance* is essential, to feel that you belong somewhere, and can relate in an intimate way to someone special. Family, friends, colleagues, neighbours can all play a part in assuring the person that he is important. Therefore they care. The utter aloneness of the self which feels unwanted, unloved and perhaps unlovable is fertile soil for the development of pathology. God created us with this need to share. Adam's existence was "not good" without Eve. This is far more than a sexual need, the emphasis in Scripture is on companionship, on having a helper "fit for him". This need to share oneself with another is as important as the need to eat. Loneliness is the inability to share. That is why a person can be lonely in a crowd of people. Sharing is scary because it always involves the reality of rejection. Yet a person cannot be accepted if he is not willing to take the risk of being rejected, by sharing himself with another. Thus a fear of rejection produces a life style of loneliness. Rejection may·be temporarily painful, but loneliness is a slow form of psychological suicide.

Accomplishment is the second basic psychological need. If unfulfilled, this need will lead to psychological illness. It is the need to struggle, to plan ahead, to battle toward a difficult goal, and then to enjoy the conquest. Crucial to its fulfilment is the disciplined use of one's time and an awareness of one's priorities. Without some degree of accomplishment in one's behaviour, a feeling of helplessness develops. Accomplishment occurs only through struggle. This negates the idea that struggle and even suffering are bad: rather to struggle in the midst of suffering can create a psychologically healthy person. But it is also important to see some results. Stress can best be coped with whenever the consequences are seen to have an ultimate purpose. If a struggle is perceived as useless, then the person sees himself as helpless in it. Sometimes it means that a saint of God will simply trust God to work out the purpose in his pain. This is not a form of martyrdom. Rather it is a deliberate commitment to God to control the present distress and to enable the person to learn from it. Such learning is a concrete result which then encourages more coping, strength leading to strength.

In the realm of the spirit, there are three basic needs which if met promote health, if unmet produce disease. They are: worship, warfare and witness. *Worship* is simply the adoration of the eternal. But what is seen as eternal differs. In essence it should be communication with God, but different people create their own particular gods. For any abstract value can be adored as if it were *the* source of all being. Thus, truth, beauty, wisdom, justice, unity, order, life are all examples of abstract (eternal) values that appeal to the need to worship something. These may take on more temporal aspects to become respectively the career-related 'gods' of education, art, teaching, law, arbitration, administration, and medicine. The distinction between health and disease is very subtle here: if these values or these careers remain as goals of life it is healthy, but if they become gods in an obsessional way it is unhealthy. A basic principle emerges: whatever you worship, that is what you become. Therefore be careful what you do worship! The need to worship is so intense that everyone worships someone or something. Perhaps the biggest danger here is an introspection that ends up in self-worship. This self-love leads to self-destruction. But an adoration of Christ, where he becomes the centre of one's being, produces a person who is able "to be made new in the attitude of your minds, and to put on the new self, created to be like God in true righteousness and holiness" (Ephesians 4:23-24). Thus, to worship the Lord is to become like him in character and personality.

Warfare is the second spiritual need which must be fulfilled. Warfare is the need to engage in conflict with internal sins and external evil. Spiritual realities demand spiritual battles. These can be more demanding than all the psychological and physical battles combined. In Ephesians, the Christian is told to stand against the devil's schemes, against the spiritual forces of evil in the heavenly realms — all in the power of God (Ephesians 6:10-18). The usual arena for this battle is prayer, a prayer in the Spirit which applies the victory of the Cross of Christ to "extinguish all the flaming arrows of the evil one". This intense prayer is agonising — a spiritual wrestling match! Yet from this spiritual exercise, new strength is gained to fulfil the purposes of God. What a mystery this is! That God, in his sovereignty, should choose to delegate spiritual power to the Christian to be used in warfare. If this warfare is avoided, then not only are the specific battles lost temporarily, but the spiritual nature of that Christian remains stagnant. This stagnation can often be the first step toward disobedience in other areas. Prayer thus becomes a barometer in the person of spiritual health or disease. To be healthy the Christian needs to be strengthened in his spirit as a prayer warrior.

The need to *witness* is like the need for warfare. In warfare there is an unseen but real battle, often known only to God and the devil. But in witness, the need is for a public exercise of spiritual power. It is the communication of the gifts and fruit of the Spirit (Galatians 5:22) to the church. The danger of spiritual disease is present here too. If the person refuses to give his gift or apply his fruit for the good of the whole, both lose out on a blessing. Whenever a gift is unused, a potential unrealised, it produces frustration in the personality leading to imbalance. This imbalance may begin with the failure to witness of the individual Christian, but it will infect the entire body of believers (1 Corinthians 12:26).

Disease or imbalance in the personality may be the result of either specific distortions or unfulfilled needs. By looking at the complexities of human personality through the perspective of God's pattern, some of these complexities can be understood. Knowledge plus discernment is a powerful combination for a Christian counsellor.

Points for Discussion

1   Why is it so difficult to define normal and abnormal behaviour? In what way may the Scripture be used as criteria for this purpose?

2   What are the suggested parts and purposes of the body, mind and spirit in a human personality? How are these parts co-ordinated?

3   How may the different sources of illness within the person be identified? Which ones may the Christian counsellor deal with, and which ones should be referred to a more competent counsellor/doctor?

4   Why is it essential in counselling to be sure of the source of the problem? How is it possible to become sure of the source?

5   In what way is balance the key to fulfilment of basic needs within the person? How may an unmet need produce frustration and imbalance?

6   Which basic physical, psychological and spiritual needs are largely unmet in yourself?

7   What is the role of Christian fellowship (including exhortation and confrontation) in helping to fulfil these basic needs in a counsellor? In what way is the effectiveness of the counsellor dependent upon this personal need fulfilment?

CHAPTER FIVE

Age-Behaviour Relationships

BEHAVIOUR is always evaluated according to one's age. Thus, a lack of concentration in a five-year-old is considered 'normal', in a thirty-year-old it would be 'abnormal', and in an eighty-year-old it is 'normal' again. Counselling involves a constant evaluation of what specific behaviours are 'normal' or 'abnormal'. Thus, it is necessary to have some knowledge of the types of problems related to specific periods in development. The counsellor must look at any psychological problem from the context of the person's age at its onset. Because behaviour is always related to age, when the expected problems for each age level are understood by the counsellor, they provide a realistic foundation for effective counselling.

Throughout the life span, each person is continually changing, yet remains the same. This is the paradox of human personality. It means that: (1) the core of a person's identity is present from birth to death, as an unchanging framework for each subsequent behaviour; and (2) the possibility of change in attitudes is constant, as a limitless number of new behaviours are learned. So as the individual grows older, his core personality is constant, while his attitudes and/or actions are always changing. A child at the age of five will be the same person at the age of fifty, yet vastly different too. An awareness of these age-behaviour relationships allows the counsellor to understand the client. Therefore this chapter will focus on the expected physical and emotional changes at each major period of development.

Babyhood

From the zygote (the fertilised cell) comes a creature at physical maturity composed of about 26,000,000,000 cells. This phenomenal cell division is most accelerated during the foetal life before birth, but continues as each type of tissue renews itself throughout the lifetime of the individual. Each cell must 'know' when to divide into two daughter cells and when to stop this division. This division is controlled by a genetic code in each cell — the DNA. It is the DNA which controls the degree and duration of physical changes in the person. Genetically each person is unique. The DNA builds the biological uniqueness into each person. Identical twins are the only exception. Identical twins do have the same hereditary background (DNA) but they do not have the same environment — either before or after birth. It is correct to state, therefore, that each person is totally unique: created by God for a distinct purpose and comparable to no-one else, either physically, emotionally or spiritually.

During the foetal life of the individual, this uniqueness begins. The DNA code determines when and how the ectoderm is to develop into skin and nerve tissue, the mesoderm is to become bone and muscle tissue, and the endoderm is to divide into the digestive organs. From about the fourth week after conception, the heart is formed and begins pulsating the rhythm of life. For the mother, the foetal age of five months is significant, since this is when the baby begins to move and/or kick within the womb. This allows the mother to 'feel' something of the mystery of a life being created within her.

Yet the connection, both physically and psychologically, between the mother's life and the baby's life has been there since conception through the placenta. This is the tissue that connects the foetus to the mother's blood supply in order to transmit needed nutrients and antibodies to the developing baby, and to take away the accumulated waste products. The placenta acts as a filter too, for only specific substances may pass its barriers to affect the foetus. One of the chemicals in the mother's blood which does pass through the filtering system of the placenta is the stress hormone ACTH. This means that the psychological state of the mother is physically transmitted to the foetus. The higher the mother's stress level during pregnancy, the greater amount of ACTH in her bloodstream to influence the baby's development. ACTH is the stress hormone because it accelerates the body's physiology for necessary action during stress. The anxiety level of the mother is raised as a part of this preparation for stress, but because of the connection in the placenta — anxious mothers produce anxious babies. As ACTH stimulates the foetus beyond the normal limits, the foetus becomes over-stimulated before birth and a more anxious baby after birth. This anxiety may be manifested in excessive movements (hyperactivity), poor sleeping or eating behaviour, and/or excessive crying in the newborn. This is but another example of the psychological-physical interdependence within the person.

But, in application, it is a fact of biology which a counsellor needs to know in order to interpret accurately a young child's anxious behaviour to an anxious parent. Why would a one-year-old continue to scream and sleep poorly? First, medical reasons should be thoroughly investigated as a possible cause. But there may be a psychological cause too, as the mother's anxiety before the baby's birth over-stimulated his physiology. Now after birth, if the mother continues to be anxious, this tension will be transmitted via the sense of touch to the newborn. Through both the physical and psychological channels, the anxiety is 'catching'. Therefore, during pregnancy some supportive counselling of the mother may be mandatory to reduce her fears and/or anxiety; while, after the birth of the child, an explanation of his anxious behaviours may help the mother in coping with the problem. Such an explanation need not produce guilt in the mother. Rather, once someone cares enough to counsel the mother, her tension is relieved and the baby's anxiety is reduced as well. Of course, the mother's anxiety may itself have many sources, each of which should be untangled. Having a baby is a normal and wonderful event, but it often triggers off abnormal emotions from the past experiences of the parents.

For the child, infancy is a time of rapid learning. He reacts to the amount and type of stimuli coming at his developing sense organs, all the lights, sounds, tastes, smells and touches of a new and mysterious world. Since these organs are still in the process of development, much of the information transmitted through them is distorted or incomplete. People's faces are seen as big blurs at first, only sweet and sour tastes are perceived, and loud noises get the biggest reaction regardless of their meaning. The most developed, and hence most accurate, sense is that of touch. The tactile cells receive and transmit to the brain of the infant the basic information of his new world. In fact, they work well enough to tell the infant what is happening (is it wet or cold?), who is holding him (are they anxious or loving?), and how he likes it (it feels good or bad). Because of this communication via touch, it is essential to demonstrate love as often as possible to the infant.

Psychologically, the sense of touch is the way trust is communicated to the infant. According to the psychologist Erik Erikson, it is during this first year of life that a child learns either basic trust or mistrust toward others in his environment (Erikson, 1963). The development of trust or mistrust is learned through an association with the consistent care (trust) or inconsistent care (mistrust) given by the mother. If when he is wet or hungry he cries, and consistently mother comes to relieve the problem, then the child internalises an attitude of trust. Trust is a basic belief that next time appropriate help will come. Conversely, if his needs are met by a different person or in inconsistent ways by the same person, mistrust will be learned. As a result the child will expect to be disappointed (mistrust) in future situations and/or people. This learning is non-verbal in the child, yet its consequences continue into adult life as the person either expects others to help him (trust) or hurt him (mistrust).

All through that child's life his/her psychological capacity to relate to people will be dependent upon the degree of developed trust. Trust is a prerequisite for love. Therefore, all close relationships to people (beginning with parents, generalising to friends), will be shaped by the security or insecurity of the first relationship to a person — usually the mother. In the extreme case, where a newborn is put into a foundling home, or orphanage, and cared for by many different and inconsistent nurses ('mothers'), there will always be psychological damage, including the possibility of death. The inability to trust specific people is one symptom of psychological illness in an adult which may also come from such an early background of emotional neglect. In general, the quality and consistency of love given to an infant forms the foundation of all future psychological learning.

There are spiritual consequences to the development (or non-development) of trust within the psyche as well. If an individual really believes that others cannot be trusted, then he cannot reach out to accept their love and remains isolated. When a child has not lived with a sense that he is loved, soon he is frustrated, angry and may even think that he is not capable of being loved at all. If the message of God's love in Christ is presented to such a child or adolescent, how can he accept on a spiritual level what has not been experienced first on a human level? Such a young person may in fact feel angry at the mere mention of God loving him, when no-one else has ever loved him before. There is a deficit in this person's development of trust which blocks relationships of love towards others. But without a capacity to trust people, he cannot believe in or trust God's love either. Therefore, the first year of life, when this attitude of trust is learned, constitutes a critical period for the development of both psychological and spiritual relationships.

What happens if trust is not learned during the first year of life? Does it limit the person to a lifetime of isolation from people and God? No! A real ability to trust can be learned as an adolescent, or even as an adult. The later in life it is done, the more difficult it will be to first unlearn previous attitudes — but it can be done. When there are caring people, or a caring counsellor, trust can be learned in adulthood too. When the caring is genuine, even though tested by the client's rejection of the counsellor, this will allow the later development of trust. The counselling process gives opportunity to discuss these early childhood relationships and their effect upon personality development. Counselling can likewise give encouragement for the person to begin to trust others because he has now received love.

Childhood

From the age of exploration known as toddlerhood (3-4 years old), comes the visual image of a cherub. They may look angelic, but their behaviour is not! Since everything is exciting at this age, it needs to be explored via doing. The child learns by his/her actions, which are often repetitions to check up on what was learned.

Thinking in this stage is very 'autistic' (self-centred) so that literally the child's thoughts revolve around himself alone. Thus, if he is sleepy, hungry, playful, bored, etc. — everyone else is too. This is why if the toddler wakes up at 6 a.m. on Sunday and wants to play, his parents should want to play too! What a delightful self-centredness this is. Most parents tolerate it by allowing the child to do what he wants sometimes, and then at other times they also impose limits of authority where the child must conform to another's standards. Some three to four year olds can be very stubborn as well as selfish. The absolute authority of the parent in certain areas will be easier for the child to learn if he is secure in their love. But submission to the love and discipline of the parent should be firmly established at this age in order to avoid problems later.

By the time a child reaches the age of five or six, verbal ability has developed to the point of rapid learning about his environment. Questions may abound about the meaning of their experiences — "Why does the sun come up each morning?", or "Who made the grass to be green?" This is the time when experience can be just as real within (via imagination and thought) as it is without (via exploration and action). It is usually a pleasant surprise to a child when he realises that no-one else can know his thoughts — they are his alone. Yet this same fact often produces guilt too, for he will think about "how nice it would be to throw baby brother out of the window" and immediately feel the shame of having such a secret thought.

Thoughts often equal reality to a child. If in imagination a violent act is planned, then there is the consequence of guilt — as though it were done in reality. This is probably when repression of feelings begins, in order to cope with such strong guilt feelings within. So the very private world of thought becomes for the five-to-six-year old the arena of his greatest pleasure (in imagination) and his greatest pain (in guilt feelings). Often the parents are not aware of how sensitive and secretive their child's life really is. It is during this age, therefore, that a child should learn how to share his feelings. This will prevent the process of repression from becoming the habitual way of coping with stress. But there must be a parent or another adult in the home who is willing to listen to both the fantasy and fear of the child.

It is during the four to six age period that sexual curiosity and fantasies may confuse the thinking of the child. Again, if there is no-one to share these with, the confusion produced will often be repressed only to be later expressed in adult sexual problems. Role identification should be learned at this age level: a girl should be able to identify with the mother (wanting to be like her in behaviour) so that she learns what it is like to be a woman. The four-year-old boy likewise will need to be like his father, imitate his actions, and thereby learn what being a man is all about.

Usually this is the process of sex-role learning: from imitation comes identification. The parent of the same sex as the child is the model to be imitated, and the child then generalises to believe that if "Daddy fixes things when they break, all men should do this", or if "Mom screams each time she does not get her own way, then all women do this". (Obviously such assumptions may be wrong, but they are nevertheless woven into the fabric of the child's fantasy regarding what a man or woman is like.) But the more male-orientated the father is (by being aggressive yet approachable), and the more female-orientated the mother is (by being submissive yet sensitive), the healthier the role models will be for the child to imitate. Dominant mothers and weak fathers as models help to confuse the sex-role learning for the child, and may contribute to psychological problems in adulthood.

Once a child is in the six to eleven-year period, there is a dominance of school and academic pursuits. Now the thinking capacity is accelerating its development, and thinking includes reasoning (from which arguing and condemning may come).

The logical ability of a nine-year-old is very precise; black is always black and white is always white. His categories by which people and things are understood are absolute; thus his morals are also absolute and the guilt from violating these standards may be absolute too. If an eight to nine-year-old does something which he knows to be wrong because his own absolute standards condemn him, but there is no punishment forthcoming from a parent — then he is trapped by his own guilt. This guilt is repressed and then later in childhood it is often expressed in inferiority feelings.

Because of a growing intellectual ability, the emotional sensitivity of the child may be less evident. The child thinks and learns about all the academic aspects of living, from basic grammar to allow communication, to the mathematical tables to quantify concepts — these will dictate his development. The school and the pressure of peers is great during this period. Often a child may deliberately be 'bad' while in school just to avoid the censure of his peers for possibly becoming the "teacher's pet". Thus there is an emotional sensitivity still, but it is directed towards social outlets, particularly towards the approval of his same sexed peers.

Another area of high emotionality during the six to eleven

period relates to feelings of inferiority. The original context may be academic, where ridicule in the classroom and/or comparison to a smarter sibling in the home combine to make the youngster feel stupid. Then a psychological principle goes into action: once you feel stupid, you begin to act stupidly. Soon this child cannot fit in with his peers, who may call him by derogatory names, nor can he relate comfortably to his family, who may pressure him into doing more than is reasonable. The 'absolute' thinking categories help to reinforce this feeling of being totally wrong; if he is 'stupid' in mathematics, then by applying absolute categories for each person, the child sees his whole self as being 'stupid'. The converse also works during this age period: for if the child has one area of superiority (sport, music, etc) this can also generalise into a total feeling of self-worth. Encouragement from concerned parents to develop an area of specific strength and minimise an area of inherent weakness can contribute to this self-worth. In this way, inferiorities during these childhood years may be overcome.

Adolescence and Young Adulthood

In primitive societies there is a quick transition via 'rites of passage' from childhood to adulthood. But the more advanced a society becomes, the longer the period of transition extends. Adolescence is the era of continuing change; while young adulthood is an era of commitments to work and marriage.

Adolescence is a very difficult period physically and psychologically because of the tension created from change itself. Physically, the body of the adolescent is outwardly changing before his eyes. A growth spurt may begin the teen-age years, so that new clothes are necessary and everyone mentions how tall he has become. The self-consciousness of the teenager can be intense; he just wants to crawl into a hole and hide until all the physical changes are over — but he cannot find a hole big enough! Psychologically, he feels trapped within a body that is not his, with new moods almost each day. Emotional over-reaction is the norm for a teenager. One day he will scream about how ugly he is due to two blotches on his face (from acne), and the next day he will be stoic about the pain of a broken arm (from football)!

The physical changes in adolescence are most acute during

puberty. For a boy, this is about the age of twelve to thirteen; while for a girl, puberty begins at eleven or twelve usually. It is essentially the sexual maturation stage where the whole hormonal balance alters to produce a physical structure capable of reproducing itself.

In boys, their voice pitch lowers, the genital organs enlarge in size, a beard begins and finally sperm is found in the urine. About the age of fifteen, the manufacture of sperm is so numerous that an outlet is found via ejaculations while asleep or 'wet dreams'. Since all of these changes are known to the boy, there is often much comparison done with other males going through the same experiences — just to reassure each that such reactions are shared, hence normal. These verbal comparisons may become exaggerated claims of male powers, that are used to intimidate the shy or late developing male in the peer group. Such camaraderie may be a healthy way of accepting one's own maleness by first accepting another male as a friend, or it may develop into a homosexual exploration.

Mutual masturbation between boys in their early teens is a common phenomenon and does *not* indicate the beginning of a homosexual lifestyle. However, since the erratic feelings attached to the act are strangely new (even frightening), there is a definite need for the boy to be able to talk over these feelings with a more mature male. Discussion is needed about the adolescent's latent fear of homosexuality, or misunderstandings regarding heterosexuality. These are deeply disturbing issues for the adolescent and should be clarified within a Christian context.

The sex drive reaches its peak in males about the age of seventeen to eighteen. An intense physical need for release may lead the teenager into many forms of sex-related behaviour, from masturbation to rape. The tension of physically needing a sexual outlet but socially being denied such an outlet before marriage, is the dilemma of a seventeen-year-old boy. As the sexual tension increases within, so does the fear that self-control cannot be maintained. Perhaps this is one reason why the male mind is able to rationalise here, and after indulging in some sex-related experience (in fantasy or reality) can then easily divorce that experience from any emotion of love. So an isolated sex relationship (homosexual and/or heterosexual) may be just an experimentation — not an emotional commitment for a young

man. It may symbolise physical release not emotional fulfilment. But if these feelings are not shared with someone else who
understands, they can become the beginning of a distorted
sexual image.

Sexually, the development of girls from puberty through
adolescence is structured quite differently. The first physical
sign of emerging sexuality is usually the menarche. It is a
definite monthly reminder of her female uniqueness, and physically often becomes a barometer of the psychological degree of
acceptance of that biological role. With a healthy, even joyous
awareness of her new potential for motherhood, there is often a
painless cycle; but with an unhealthy, even bitter acknowledgement of her potential motherhood, then there is more likely to
be a painful menstruation. This is another example of the
psychological affecting the physical aspects of the person.

In the teenage girl, the psychological always seems to
dominate the physical aspects of her sexuality. Sheer sexual tension is rarely experienced, rather romantic and/or maternal
feelings may be easily aroused. Thus, sex is primarily linked
with love, and without the emotional involvement of love
sexual exploration is uncommon. Because of this difference
from the male sexual make-up, promiscuous behaviour in a
teenage girl is more serious. More disturbed girls may use their
sexual powers as a weapon of revolt against a parent or against
themselves (perhaps to prove their inferiority anew). Another
frequent motive for promiscuity in girls is to seek for love via
sex. If the sixteen-year-old feels unwanted by her parents, aca-
demically inferior at school and generally without any direction
toward any career goal — then sexual submission is seen as the
only hope of finding some kind of love. Surely there is an urgent
need for teenage girls to be able to discuss and better understand
their emerging sexual feelings prior to such experimentation.
Christian counsellors and/or parents should be available and
trained enough to put these problems into a proper perspective.

One interesting fact regarding female sexuality is that it
reaches its peak at about the age of thirty years. This, too, is
vastly different from the male sex drive, and has its consequences whether the young woman is married or not. If she is a
wife, her rather sudden increased desire for sex may perplex
(even delight) her husband; but if she is unmarried, then the
social pressure to be so plus the strong sex drive within may pre-

cipitate an unwise union. A Christian young woman of thirty is in need of special social and spiritual support in order to cope with this tension. A caring Christian fellowship, where her frustration can be shared and understood is essential.

On the emotional plane, the development of teenage boys and girls is more parallel. Both sexes during their mid to late adolescence go through the classic struggle known as 'identity crisis'. There are many types of pressure for the adolescent: physical changes, different social and/or familial expectations, and the emotional moodiness within. As a result, the average teenager usually finds himself in the middle of nowhere. This is a lonely, often desperate place of despair, where no-one else can come to lead the young person out of himself. Exciting activity may be a mask to cover up this inner desperation, but whenever the activity stops, the empty core of a self emerges again. Essentially, the identity crisis is not knowing where you belong, or where you should be going, or why. It is summarised in this question: Who am I?

Identity has many meanings. Basically, identity is a process. The good experiences from the past (one's roots) are combined with the expectations for the future (one's goals) to produce a sense of self-worth. This self-worth is the basis for an ongoing awareness of self — an identity. Thus, roots plus goals equal worth, and from this self-worth, identity emerges.

This formula may seem simple to apply, but often it is not. First, the past experiences of the young person may leave little positive memories to incorporate into a self-image; and secondly, there may be few realistic goals for the young person to aim at in to-day's society. So if you do not like where you have come from and cannot plan ahead to know where you are going, how can self-worth be developed? The answer may be found within a Christian counselling context. For the counsellor should be able to help the person to realise how much the Lord was involved (actively protecting and preventing) in each event in the person's past. Indeed, for the Christian, "all things work together for good" (Romans 8:28), and this includes early childhood experiences. Likewise, God is in charge of all future events. God even plans specific things for each Christian to do (Ephesians 1:1, 2:10, Romans 12:6). Therefore, there must be a future for the individual Christian that is good and acceptable to that person (Romans 12:1-2). When a young person realises that the Lord has loved him enough to guide him into each experience, and that this same love is preparing future tasks just for him — how can he not but feel a deep sense of personal worth?

A person's identity needs time to develop. Interests are explored and dropped, new opportunities are followed up, all in the confidence that God is in charge of each 'door' that opens or closes. Even in the midst of frustrations and delays, if encouragement keeps coming, the young person can continue to develop strengths of character which are a part of the sense of self.

Vocational and marital commitments are two significant consequences of an emerging identity that may begin in late adolescence or early adulthood. In fact, these two choices (of a job and a mate), are the results of an awarenes of who is doing the choosing. For by what he does, the young person affirms what he is. Once an identity is known, it includes some sense of strengths and weaknesses in both what you do (vocational awareness) and to whom you relate best (marital selection). But without an accurate identity awareness, these significant decisions will most often be wrong for the particular personality of the individual. Psychologically, the consequences can be devastating: the person finds himself in a job he cannot enjoy and married to a person he cannot love.

Young adulthood is the loneliest of all periods of development. This is because the emotional ties have been loosened toward the family of birth, but they have not yet become attached to a new family via marriage. The young adult is in a state of psychological limbo. The frustration of this state may precipitate an early union — as an impulsive attempt to end the loneliness of belonging to no-one. This loneliness is made even worse if the person lives alone in a larger city where employment and/or educational possibilities are greater and then jumps from one job/college to another in a ruthless scramble for success. Each step forward is seen as futile without someone with whom to share it. Perhaps the desperation of loneliness builds up until belonging to someone for any reason (including just sex) is better than emptiness.

Then the desperation experienced by the young person before marriage may become depression within marriage. For, if the hoped-for solution to instability or loneliness fails, what else is left? Disappointments in marriage are inevitable. Often they stem from a false premise such as — love gives meaning automatically to life. When this falseness is realised, it can generate either an active cycle of divorce and remarriage or a passive withdrawal into depression. The rate of divorce is very high in the late twenties and early thirties. Often the young adult cannot conceive that the problem may be within rather than without. It is always easier to project the blame on to the marriage partner, the job tensions, or even the high rate of inflation! If he/she stops long enough to look within, or is in a depressive state where too much introspection has already occurred, then a need for counselling may be recognised. If Christian counselling is available during this turbulent time, much further chaos may be prevented for the young person.

Any choice is the result of the work of the intellect. It is during the period of mid to late adolescence (sixteen to nineteen years) that the intellect is dominated by idealism. The adolescent is an impatient idealist. Abstract thinking is now fully developed, and is translated into an absolute passion for positive ideals like love, freedom, purity, and an equally strong glorification of negative states such as violence, cynicism and war.

According to the adolescent's moral standards, as internalised in the conscience, he is a perfectionist. But his attraction to (and even indulgence in) violence and sex may violate these high standards. As a result, the adolescent feels guilty; this guilt is manifested in self-hate. Idealism leads him to believe that if love is real it should control behaviour, if peace is real it should unite nations, and if purity is real one should not be able to sin. Yet he cannot be perfect in deed or thought but his intellect demands perfection. This inner contradiction of ideals may lead to extremes in both moods and manners. One day he will be kind, the next day cruel; one day policemen will be seen as all virtuous, the next as all corrupt, etc. The basic issue is that logically the adolescent cannot see how good and evil can co-exist within himself.

Some resolution of this dilemma can be found on a spiritual level of experience. Many adolescents can see that the Gospel of Christ explains how evil (man's potential for sin) has been dealt with by good (Christ's death on the cross). Neither good nor evil is obliterated within man's nature, but because of God's act, justice has been achieved. The adolescent begins to see how evil crucified good, but God's love and justice triumph eternally. Also the daily struggle with sin and the need for forgiveness is a Christian answer which makes sense to the adolescent's logic. For these reasons many adolescents are intellectually attracted to the Gospel, and by the power of the Holy Spirit many are converted at this age. Christianity makes sense out of their idealism!

However, idealism may also lead the adolescent into the opposite spiritual dimension. Evil is seen as abstract and alluring, and shown in Satanic cults. When the identity confusion emotionally combines with the intellectual fascination with evil, a commitment to Satan rescues the individual from his own nothingness. By an identification with evil, the adolescent identity achieves the status of standing for something powerful. Mystical adherence to the rituals of Satanic worship likewise helps to satisfy the adolescent's need to communicate via symbols. Rebellion against the 'hypocrisy' of parents and society may be successfully demonstrated through a liaison with 'pure' evil in a Satanic cult.

Commitment of self to something or someone helps to confirm one's identity. This makes adolescence and young adulthood a very vulnerable time. Searching for something important, that is strong enough to define oneself through, is the emotional and intellectual quest of the person. Much of the restlessness and irresponsibility shown during this period is just a consequence of this search within. In its most severe form, the restlessness may lead to withdrawal. If psychologically there is a predisposition to mental illness, it may increase the withdrawal to produce the main psychological disorder of young adulthood — schizophrenia. The Gospel must be seen by the young person as relevant to his needs, or there may be a deliberate turning towards the occult and/or psychological withdrawal. In adolescence, it is easier to have a negative identity than no identity at all.

Middle Age

After the emotional pressure to find oneself in adolescence and prove oneself in young adulthood is over, then the time of middle age comes. Middle age has its own unique quest, "What do I want out of life now that I'm doing what I ought to do?" This question comes from a persistent feeling of wanting to be 'something more' before it is too late. This is the crisis of middle age. In our modern society, this crisis is intensified as youth is glorified and age is seen only as a disability. How can you grow old and enjoy the process when the media conditions you to believe that only the young are of any value? Social roles and emotional reactions to oneself must each adjust to the fact that youth is now gone.

During the decade of the thirties, commitments are either altered or deepened. There may be the beginning of a new job, and/or a serious review of the strength of the marriage. Generally, it is a time of high creativity — both professionally and at home.

For a male in his thirties, the growth is most likely to be in a career area. He wants to excel professionally to prove (in part) that he is *not* going to make the same mistakes in a job that his father did. For a female in her thirties, the development is more likely to be home-orientated. She wants to apply her maternal abilities while often considering (or beginning) an outside career too. Both marriage partners are so busy developing their respective areas of expertise, that they realise slowly how far apart they have drifted emotionally. The husband may become attracted to the slimmer, more intellectual women at the office, yet be personally threatened by the prospect of his own wife returning to school and/or work to become like them. This tension may produce a gnawing idea that there is something wrong with the marriage. Each partner must learn how to communicate his/her feelings — or the tension will be repressed into a distorted general anxiety. Life becomes more complicated in the external things (mortgages, children's schooling, home repairs etc.) and so experience of anxiety grows. Often the attempted way of escape from these tensions during the thirties ·is to become busier and busier.

Far too soon the forties arrive. Sometimes they come with a shock, always they become the deadline decade for starting any major change in lifestyle. Youth can no longer be used as an excuse for inefficiency. By now the person is supposed to know what he is doing. But what if he does not yet know? Or what if the goal of success (at a career or home) has been achieved but there is no satisfaction in it?

These tensions may find their summation in a spiritual crisis: a re-appraisal of oneself. In the light of what is meaningful beyond the moment, something eternal must be sought and found. Why? Because the decay and disappointment of temporal things is far too evident. There are two possible solutions to this spiritual crisis. Either the individual struggles and finds meaning through a commitment to Christ, or some philosophical system of belief; or the person creates a stronger mask of superiority to cover up the misery of success without meaning. With either choice the calm exterior of the individual may suddenly change as a result of this agonising re-appraisal. Alcoholic consumption, promiscuous behaviour, compulsive buying sprees, fadish diets and clothes, adventure-like trips, and an erratic irresponsibility — all these may be symptoms of the inner struggle going on. Humanly speaking, it may be the best time to reach the person (since adolescence) with the reality of Christ. Or if one of these personal problems makes counselling necessary, it is likewise important to confront the client with his diversionary tactics which distort his inner inadequacy. Since the real problem is a spiritual one, Christian orientated counselling is needed. Through such counselling the individual can find meaning beyond himself — for both temporal and eternal dimensions.

The process of letting go can be more painful psychologically than learning to hold on to someone or something. This is the major task of the fifties — to learn to let go of dreams, physical abilities and one's own children. A practical 'orientation to the now' emerges, as the person focuses on what is possible to enjoy in the present context.

Dreams of great financial and/or business success if not achieved by the fifties decade, probably will never be realised. Since dreams serve as motives to keep going on, when the dream dies, the motive must change. Usually there is a shift in emphasis, from striving to succeed for oneself, to striving in order to care for others.

A humanitarian interest may predominate, even in the non-Christian, who now seeks to give not get. Because there is much physical energy left, the fifty-year-old has a great need to give of himself, and much personal hurt if the giving is not received. The important things become people and/or eternal values like family, friends and children. Ironically, the individual who was too busy to care in the forties, now wants to care! This may take some learning, and in some cases (as after a divorce) it is too late. It is also a particularly poignant time for another problem: the empty nest syndrome. For just when the desire is to relate to one's family more, the children are grown up and gone. As compensation, there may be grandchildren nearby, but if not, the desperate 'need to give' may put unfair pressure on a grown-up child to marry and have children. Or else there may be the tendency to interfere in the life of others — family or friends alike. In women, there may be a post-menopausal zest, and in men there is often some eccentric behaviour — all due to the emotional consequences of hormonal changes in the late forties and early fifties. This is but another area of letting go, this time of one's reproductive capacities. The real question to be answered is, what is then left to live for? Most individuals in their fifties would answer — people. However, if they have poor histories of relating to others, there may be a need to learn how to care for others. A counselling relationship can provide the chance to learn this, because in it someone first cared for them.

Old Age

When old age begins is always uncertain. It is usually determined more by attitude than chronological age. Nevertheless, in many countries it is in the decade of the sixties when a person (often still strong and able) is forced to retire. Yet in a paradoxical way, the sixties are also the decade for renewal.

Energy levels may still be high during the sixties and there is an intensity which gives meaning to each event. Any activity which has had to be postponed previously must be considered now or never. For this reason, the unselfishness of the fifties becomes the selfishness of the sixties. A longed-for home in a warmer climate, a trip to the other side of the world, an earned university degree — all these and more may be done during the sixties. As more and more friends move away or die, the sixties can also be a time of loneliness — loneliness covered up by vigorous activity.

The crisis of retirement affects both husband and wife alike. If the man defined his own worth via work, and now cannot work again — of what value is he to himself? Or if work activities kept the couple from relating to each other, what are they to do when all they have is each other? They are strangers living together, but they cannot share. As a consequence, there may be new problems for this period — for either husband or wife — ranging from sudden physical ailments to suicide. On the positive side, if the marriage has inherent strengths, then retirement may provide the time to build upon those strengths. Wisdom from experience plus love from years of commitment to each other can make this time beautiful for all. As Christians, the couple can have much to give by word and example within the Church. However, they must remember that age does not make one wise in an infallible way!

This teaching via action and precept can continue in a church and family context into the decade of the seventies. Life must now become simpler. Physical abilities and social responsibilities will be less — and the person most often is faced with living alone (Ecclesiastes 12:1-8).

A seventy-year-old is reminded daily of his limitations, in sight, sound, taste and enjoyment. The external world generally dims and the person distrusts his own sensations. Some seventy-year-olds may be pre-occupied with health and/or disease as a reaction to the accelerated aging process within. Somewhat like that of the teenager, the body is changing so fast that it demands a new definition of self. Then if the spouse should die, after many married years, how do you relate to everything all alone? This bereavement may produce a profound depression. Most certainly there is the anxiety of drastic change. Learning to be dependent on others again, but without the support of someone to share the frustration — this is the major task of the seventies. This frustration may help to foster senility in this decade or in the next. Conversely, the more independence that can be maintained by the person, the less likely it is that senility will occur.

Once the eighties and nineties have been reached, the various crises combine to produce either a state of dignity or despair. Looking backward on life can highlight certain accomplishments. This will sustain a sense of worth before God and man — and the person maintains an inner dignity. For the Christian, even the many sins can be understood as long forgiven (Psalm 104:33; Psalm 32), the hurts as beneficial to learning (Joel 2:25, Romans 8:28) and the future alive with the certainty of life after this life (Psalm 46, 2 Corinthians 5:1-10).

However, if the person cannot be assured by these truths, because of psychological and/or spiritual bondage, then an absolute despair may dominate. If the person feels unwanted by man and forsaken by God, where can he turn for help at age eighty-five? The despair is a realistic reaction to the futility of a life that never sought or found meaning in the Lord.

> "Do not be deceived: God cannot be mocked. A man reaps what he sows. The one who sows to please his sinful nature, from that nature will reap destruction; the one who sows to please the Spirit, from the Spirit will reap eternal life." (Galatians 6:7-8)

Points for Discussion

1 How may an understanding of the expected 'normal' behaviours for each chronological period help in evaluating the problems of a client? *Normal vs. Abnormal*

2 In what ways does the genetic uniqueness of each individual contribute to a person's sense of worth before God?

3 Explain something of the psychological and physical effects of stress upon the pregnant mother and the foetus. How does this show why an anxious mother may have an anxious baby?

4 During the first year of life, which mode of communication (sense) is most important for receiving information about the outside world? *tactile*

5 Why is a sense of trust so basic to healthy development? According to Erikson, how is trust learned? What are the spiritual consequences of the development of trust?

6 What is the primary issue to be learned during toddlerhood? *Sub. to love + discipline*

7 In which ways does guilt play a part in the secret thoughts of a child? How could a parent or concerned adult help a child recognise and deal with guilty feelings?

8 How does a child learn to see himself as a boy (herself as a girl) or their sex-role identity? What effect does this sex-role identity have upon other aspects of development?

9 How may inferiority feelings develop in a child? In what way can a counsellor help a parent to recognise and minimise such feelings in their child?

10   What are the basic physical changes at puberty for a boy and for a girl? What are the psychological consequences of these physical changes?

11   In what ways are the physical and psychological pressures of the sex drive different for a young male and a young female? How may these differences cause problems within a teenage (or early twenties) marriage situation?

12   What is the meaning of the 'identity crisis' of young people? What emotional problems emerge if this crisis is not solved during young adulthood? How are the making of commitments (especially marital and vocational) involved in the development of an identity for a young person?

13   In what ways may the idealism of young people contribute to their emotional and spiritual perspectives of life?

14   What is the psychological crisis of middle age? How may marriage conflicts during this period be a manifestation of this middle age crisis? How may spiritual conflicts in this period become an expression of middle age concerns? How can the Christian counsellor communicate the meaning of this crisis to untangle marital and spiritual issues?

15   What are some of the psychological consequences of retirement for a husband and for the wife? What could be the role of the Church and/or Christian counsellor to support the couple during this time?

16   What are some of the fears relating to disease and death which may afflict an older person? How can a person in their seventies or eighties best be helped to deal with the death of a spouse? What is the role of the family and Church during this period of adjustment?

CHAPTER SIX

A Common Coping Approach: Defence Mechanisms

GOD knows all about us. He is omniscient, but we do not know all about ourselves. Psalm 139 emphatically states that all of our thoughts and actions are known to God, even before they occur. It concludes with a prayer by the Psalmist to be searched! "See if there is any offensive way in me and lead me in the way everlasting"; this can be done only after the Lord has tested "me and known my anxious thoughts" (Psalm 139:23-24). Why? If God knows me already why pray that he might search me? Because each person needs to know more of himself, including his anxiety.

One of the strongest of psychological forces is self-deception. Every part of the person — body, mind, spirit — becomes involved in this evasion of truth. Under hypnosis the spirit can trick the body into feeling no pain during surgery, or with the use of a 'placebo' (sugar pill) the mind believes it has received a pain-killer and the body perceives little pain. Less dramatic examples occur each day as an individual distorts the world slightly in accordance with his mental outlook. Thus, if a person is moody, on his 'happy' days all seems to go well and others like him; but on the 'bad' days nothing goes right and all others are out to reject him. In this case his expectations (which could be false) determine his responses to situations.

Definition and Purpose of Defence Mechanisms

Effective counselling must both recognise amd remove these self-deceptions. Therefore, it is essential to know what common patterns the deceptions may take. Truth can set a person free from himself only if the areas of untruth are known. The client comes with a distorted self-image. He cannot consciously discard the deceptions (distortions) until confronted with them by the counsellor. These psychological cover-ups in the client take many forms, but the most common are called defence mechanisms. It is the counsellor's responsibility to detect these specific defences before the real problems in counselling can be resolved.

A defence mechanism is simply an habitual way of maintaining distortions of either a problem or a person. Reality is seen as being too complex to cope with, so a mask is used to help make stress more bearable. This is like a psychological suit of armour, uncomfortable, heavy and cold, which is worn over the self to protect it from being wounded in life's battles. There are two types of defence mechanism. They either cover up the *problem,* so that it may be seen as less difficult to handle, or they cover up the *person,* so that he may see himself as less responsible to act in changing the situation. These protections against anxiety most often fail to achieve either purpose. Instead of reducing problems, the distortion involved makes it more difficult for the person to see the real problems or himself clearly.

These distortions of the problem or person mostly begin in childhood. They are learned by imitating the coping pattern of one's family. Each family uses (or misuses) a select number of defences which then become its accepted way of dealing with any difficult stress situation. These are never consciously recognised or discussed by the family, yet on an unconscious level, without words, they are perceived as a necessary form of self-protection. For example, one family may transfer to others responsibility for a dispute, thereby making them less responsible to deal with the argument themselves. A statement like, "he started to annoy me" is unconsciously read as, "he is to blame, not me, for the fight". Another family may teach its child to deny reality by not allowing crying as a reaction to pain with the statement, "Don't think about it and it won't hurt". Another parent may encourage his child, in a similar situation of pain, to sublimate by stating, "Just keep thinking about all the ice-cream you can eat after your tonsils are out!"

Each person learns certain patterns of protection from his family, but the degree to which he uses them is related to his own level of emotional health. The more balanced the person is psychologically, the less need there is to cope via distortion. His emotional strength allows an awareness of the real undistorted situation, and produces an ability to deal with its inherent anxiety. The converse is also true: the more disturbed the person is emotionally the more distortions will be needed in a vain attempt to cope with stress. Thus, in 'normal individuals' defence mechanisms are used occasionally; in 'neurotics' their use is more frequent, and in 'psychotics' their use is almost continual.

Types of Defence Mechanisms

The major types of defences are either attempted protections of the problem or of the person. See Figure 5 overleaf.

All defence mechanisms may be used, but it is more likely for a person to select about three or four. As stresses multiply more are used, but the person himself is not aware that the numbers (or intensity) of his distortions are increasing.

Distortions of the problem via defence mechanisms would include the following: repression; denial; displaced aggression, and reaction formation.

Repression distorts awareness of the situation, by a refusal to think about the stress in the hope that it will become less difficult over time. It is a temporary manoeuvre of 'pushing the dirt under the rug', and then hoping all will be better (cleaned up) tomorrow. Since you cannot get anxious over something you are unaware of, tension is reduced, but this tension reduction is paradoxical: even as the conscious anxiety is decreased, the unconscious anxiety is increased. This is because more energy, leading to more fatigue, develops to avoid thinking about the stress situation. The longer the repression lasts, the more intense this internal pressure becomes. It creates an inner stress that has no name; its major symptom is a feeling of anxiety. Thus a stress situation that has been avoided (repressed) is paid for many times over in the currency of the psyche — anxiety.

However, on the surface of his personality, the individual may exhibit an attitude of passivity further to cover up the anxiety. If statements such as the following are commonly used in stress, repression is at work — "Everything is all right" or, "I don't need to do anything else about the problem" or, "Things like this never bother me". If directly reminded of the stress situation, the individual using repression would consciously admit the problem, then protest that it is nothing to be excited about and promptly forget it again. Obviously, such forgetting

TYPE	NAME	DEFINITION
DISTORTIONS OF THE PROBLEM	REPRESSION	DISTORTS AWARENESS OF THE SITUATION
	DENIAL	DISTORTS THE REALITY OF THE SITUATION
	DISPLACED AGGRESSION	DISTORTS THE SOURCE OF ANGER IN THE SITUATION
	REACTION FORMATION	DISTORTS REAL PROBLEM BY EXAGGERATING THE OPPOSITE ISSUE OR FEELING
DISTORTIONS OF THE PERSON	PROJECTION	DISTORTS THE SOURCE OF THE PERSON'S FEELINGS / BEHAVIOUR
	REGRESSION	DISTORTS THE AGE (RESPONSIBILITY) OF THE PERSON
	SUBLIMATION	DISTORTS THE NEGATIVE EMOTIONS OF THE PERSON INTO POSITIVE OUTLETS
	INTELLECTUAL-ISATION	DISTORTS THE EMOTIONS OF THE PERSON INTO ABSTRACT IDEAS ONLY

Fig. 5 : **AN OUTLINE OF MAJOR DEFENCE MECHANISMS**

is unhealthy as the person is never able to admit the problem long enough to solve it.

Denial distorts the reality of the situation by a refusal to recognise the problem at all. The particular stress simply does not exist. As a consequence, there is nothing to cope with in that area. It is a more extreme reaction than repression, which acknowledges an issue then ignores it. In denial, there is no acknowledgement because even to think about the stress would be far too painful. The seriousness of this defence is seen in one common result — the senses conspire to reinforce the denial. For example, during a period of grief, the footsteps of the dead person may continue to be heard as "proof" that he has not died! Or obvious cries for help in a marriage are never heard since the marriage is working so well (?). It may take an attempted suicide to get this spouse to realise reality. Denial is a reaction of fear. It is a fear of not being able to deal with the stress; but self-confidence and support can be given in a counselling relationship to overcome the denial. 'Shock' approaches to force reality upon the client may shatter him; rather strength to accept the awful possibility (the truth) must be built into the psyche first. Once reality does enter, the denial is broken. This makes the person very vulnerable as he must now adjust to the new true situation. Vulnerability produces desperation, especially if experienced alone. Supportive counselling, by a counsellor who demonstrates real caring for the person, is crucial in this stage, when the client begins to accept rather than to deny the true situation.

Displaced aggression distorts the source of anger in the stress situation, transferring the anger to a convenient 'scapegoat'. Like any emotion, anger can be difficult to handle appropriately. Whenever someone who is loved and/or feared causes real hurt, this hurt cannot be acknowledged as coming from that person. Why? Because the consequences are dangerous psychologically. If the person is greatly loved, then the guilt of hurting him by showing one's anger is enormous. If the person is greatly feared, then the possibility of retaliation is increased. Yet the hurt has produced real anger that demands some outlet. An innocent person (scapegoat) or neutral object is used in this situation as an anger release. The classic example is of the boss who yells at his employee, who then annoys his wife, who then picks on the child, who then kicks the dog, who then bites the flea! (That flea should be avoided at all cost!) This downward spiral is an unconscious but devastating process where everyone gets hurt.

Each 'scapegoat' has two characteristics in common. First, he/she is innocent, yet attacked. This produces much additional hurt at the unfairness of the situation, and perhaps some rationalisation that somehow the attack was earned. Particularly in a child, there is a tendency to treat the criticisms of a parent as always right, therefore the child must be always wrong. Displaced aggression breeds strong inferiority feelings in a child so used as a scapegoat. Over years such a child develops a helplessness attitude, and has guilt reactions even over minor things. The adult attitude may be, "Nothing I ever do is right, so why try!" Secondly, the 'scapegoat' cannot fight back. The employee, wife, child, dog, flea, etc., could not attack and win if the order were reversed. It is a trapped position psychologically, producing a conscious awareness of helplessness. This belief, that one is helpless, may generalise into a feeling of worthlessness, which in turn develops into a neurosis and/or depression.

When a neurotic client can achieve enough insight to see himself as an innocent 'victim' this produces an emotional release. This insight can correct a faulty self-concept of helplessness. After discussing the way in which his parents used him as a scapegoat in their marital arguments, the client may suddenly exclaim — "It wasn't that my parents disliked me, it was that they could not stand each other and took it out on me!" The counselling relationship is the context in which such an insight can be gained and maintained to undo many years of hurt. But the tragedy is that the client often has to suffer for so long because of someone else's inability to handle anger.

Reaction formation distorts the real problem by an excessive expression of the opposite issue/feeling. When the true facts or feelings in a situation cannot be accepted because they are too painful, then the reverse is emphasised as a cover-up. It is a reaction to the opposite, like a smile to cover up pain, or a joke to alleviate anxiety. In pathological cases, reaction formation can be used by a mother who never wanted her child (an unacceptable feeling), so she gives excessive 'things' to that child (an acceptable reaction). Guilt would be too intense if some such cover-up were not used, and then the mother would be forced to face the fact of her hatred toward the child.

In order to know whether reaction formation is at work or not, it is necessary to look at the excessiveness of the client's reaction. Any extreme reaction indicates a reaction formation. To convince himself away from the opposite viewpoint a client may argue a point in the extreme. Any exaggerated emotional response may be indicative of the less desirable alternative. A woman who constantly denounces her boss may feel too much positive emotion for him to admit it to herself. In practical terms, counsellors must look for these excessives and suspect the reverse to be true. For in the language of a disturbed psyche, love is shown in hate, fear is found in confidence, concern is communicated in neglect, and denial may be a cover-up for desire. Specific statements like the following will reveal a process of reaction formation in the client: "My son *always* pleased me in everything he did", or "I tell my wife *each* day, without fail, how much I love her".

Distortions of the person through the use of defence mechanisms include: projection; regression; sublimation, and intellectualisation.

Projection distorts the source of the person's feelings and/or behaviour by transferring them to another. This transfer allows the person to remain an 'innocent spectator', watching to see how the other person must be judged. It is a diversionary technique to take the focus away from the person where he would be responsible to act in the situation, and put the emphasis upon another who can be made into the responsible agent. It is just easier to blame someone else. The client feels safely detached from the stress. Instead of admitting, "I am angry with him", it is easier to say, "He is angry with me".

In more disturbed individuals, projection produces paranoia too. It starts by always blaming others for one's own actions and ends up in a mistrust of the person who is blamed. Again, projection forces the person to deny his own mistrust and transfer it (convert it) into the other person's desire to harm him (paranoia). This degree of suspicion may develop to alarming proportions resulting in a psychosis. A client complains, "My husband is trying to put more and more rat poison in my food each day." Here the paranoia is combined with psychotic delusions to prevent the person from relating to anyone meaningfully. This same client may go on to say, "He would

like to see me dead." Because of her projection she cannot admit
the real situation, which is that she would like to see him dead!
This degree of projection plus paranoia makes a counselling
relationship, based on trust, very difficult to establish. Whenever projection is at work in a client, it makes counselling difficult. Projection allows the person to believe that he is unable
to change any aspect of the problem. The client assumes no
control over the situation, for with the use of projection all
responsibility is avoided. It paralyses the person into a state of
non-action, which can precipitate withdrawal into a psychosis.
Once this withdrawal is complete, any counselling attempt will
be futile. It is necessary then to recognise and confront the client
before this occurs with his/her projections. However, this
cannot be done until some genuine trust is established between
the client and counsellor. Psychological healing of the distortion
of projection must be based upon a relationship of trust.

Regression distorts the age, and hence the degree of
responsible action expected from the person. It is a defence
whereby the person refuses unconsciously to act his age and
cope with stress. Rather he reverts backward in time to an
earlier, childish mode of behaviour. This forces others to take
charge and 'rescue' him from the problem. As another bonus, it
also allows the person to get more attention due to his childlike
behaviour. If a wife sits and cries whenever the chequebook
needs to be balanced, not only will her husband be forced to
stop and do it, but she will never have the opportunity to learn
how to cope with it. Another example would be a child who at
age six reverts back to earlier attention-getting behaviour
(throwing a temper tantrum), soon after the birth of a baby
brother.

Regression often results in an attitude of helplessness when in
the midst of problem situations. The client has a fear of not
coping; he fears that he is not a responsible adult. Regression
thus leads to less and less coping with problems, and the
imagined fear becomes a reality. Then, too, the client may feel
anger toward the person who took over and coped in his place.
That other person is seen to be responsible for the current helpless state of the client — "How can I learn to cope, if I am not
allowed to try?" Or this client may add the statement, "Why
can't she let me make up my own mind instead of taking charge
of everything?" Prior to this angry outburst there was a period

of regression in this same client. One of his previous comments was: "Whenever I scream at her that is the only time she will listen to my ideas at all." The client's screaming produced attention, but was so unpleasant that his wife ended up by taking charge beforehand to prevent the screaming. While the husband resented her takeover, it was only through supportive counselling that he was enabled to see how his regression had caused his wife's behaviour in the first place.

Sublimation distorts the 'negative' emotions of the person by changing them into 'positive' outlets. As defence mechanisms go, this is one of the best (healthiest) to use. For it rechannels a negative impulse (harmful desire) into a positive action. The tension in the person is released not repressed, and the consequence is socially acceptable. Thus, a strong sex drive is sublimated or rechannelled into sports activity, or hostility is sublimated into a job involving demolition work. Sublimation is a refusal to accept one's own lustful or aggressive desires; they must be seen only in 'respectable' ways. This denial of the negative aspects of self makes the enjoyment of one's righteousness more likely.

Sublimation may thus result in a judgmental, or an 'holier than thou' attitude toward other people's weaknesses. Such a client may say about another person, "Whenever I am upset or angry, I go for a long walk in the country and feel better, so why can't he control his anger better?" Or the sublimation may be so strong that the person is unaware of ever being angry at all. This allows the client to feel superior to others. Many good things have been produced via sublimation, from great poetry to needed inventions, but it is still a distortion of the self. As long as the negative (in the Christian sense — sinful) aspects of the self are denied, they cannot be understood and/or forgiven. Unconfessed sin in a Christian client still has power to affect his spirit and through the spirit the whole personality. It is in a supportive Christian counselling relationship that a client may first be able to see his sublimation. It may take the form of compulsive church activity as the result of sublimated guilt. Once freed from this guilt, his maturation (as well as effectiveness) in Christian service will be different. It is always possible to do the right thing for the wrong reason, and the Lord is clearly more interested in the right motive. Sublimation distorts the motive, making the person acceptable in his activity but confused in his self-concept. But counselling can clarify the person's view of himself, to enable more acceptance of his own and other's weaknesses.

Intellectualisation distorts the emotions of the person by transferring them into abstract ideas only. It is a negation of the feeling capacity (emotions) and an over-emphasis upon intellect (thinking). Imbalance in the personality results from this non-development of emotions. Emotional expression is intrinsically human, but the person who intellectualises becomes more like a robot than a human being. His whole ability to communicate meaningfully with others becomes distorted, and he feels trapped in an intellectual castle of his own making. Fear is the basis of this defence, a fear of not being able to cope when the weapons are feelings, so another set of weapons, words, are used almost exclusively. This means that whenever other people counter-attack with feelings a quick withdrawal into an abstract argument is essential. Thus, intellectualisation leads to emotional isolation.

As a part of this isolation process there may be the additional rationalisation of self-righteousness. The client may state, "Others cannot communicate with me because they are not up to my intellectual level". As long as the client distorts his self-concept by believing he is superior intellectually, the emotional weakness is covered up. Such an individual may be argumentative, provoking debates on abstract (non-personal) subjects as his only comfortable method of communicating with others. Or the person may prefer books to people, until one person tries to break through and communicate on an emotional level. This may produce a panic reaction, out of fear of, and yet desire for, such an emotional relationship. Then the defence of intellectualisation is seen at last for what it is — a cover up for emotional weaknesses.

In the counselling situation, because of the client's defence of intellectualisation, he may be excessive in his words but minimal in his self-disclosure. He will give facts, but few feelings apart from an awareness of emptiness. Somewhat like an emotional retardate, the client will have to learn slowly how to recognise and responsibly express emotions. Excess words, interesting and/or argumentative digressions, must be controlled in the counselling. The focus should be kept on the feelings of the person, past and present, and his right to recognise them. Studies of the emotions and their expression in the life of Christ or Saint Paul, will appeal as an exercise to his intellect, but will also prepare the Christian client for emotional development and expression.

Relevancy of Defence Mechanisms to Christian Experience

The premise, underlying all defence mechanisms, is that reality is too difficult to deal with directly. Psychological cover-ups would be unnecessary if strengths were equal to the stress. A Christian has strength beyond himself. A Christian has at his disposal the strengths and security of God. This leads to an obvious conclusion — the Christian should have less need to employ defence mechanisms to cope with reality.

This is a valid conclusion only if the Christian is aware of and is applying the strengths from his faith. Many Christians, due to spiritual and/or psychological immaturity, are not utilising their resources. For example, they may 'use' prayer to put God on their own side of an issue, rather than to be strengthened in prayer, as submission to the sovereignty of God is achieved. Church fellowship meetings may be 'used' as a place to parade the latest gossip and thus feel temporarily superior in comparison to the conflicts/sins of others. By contrast, Church fellowships may be times of 'sharing leading to caring' among the believers. Then the Christians are strengthened as they are honest enough to share themselves and obedient enough to care for each other. Through such times of fellowship, strengths are doubled when someone is sharing a burden with you, and fears are halved if you know that you are genuinely loved as you are. This support from the brethren can even cast out the fear of not being able to cope, since no matter what stress arises the confidence will be fulfilled that someone (a Christian brother) will be there to see you through it. "Like a bridge over troubled waters", God's love will be sufficient for all stress as it is applied in his people.

In addition, there should be those within the fellowship of the Church who are especially trained in a Christian counselling ministry. These Christians need both the objectivity from a knowledge of personality, and the discernment of spiritual realities from the Holy Spirit. With the availability of such

Christian counsellors, it is possible both to prevent certain family-related problems, via marriage/family seminars, and to treat psychologically those individuals in particular distress. Again, if the average Christian knew such counselling services were an acceptable resource to use, much emotional agony could be lessened. There would be a means available for Christians to care for each other. The more a disturbed Christian realises that his Lord loves him just as he is, the easier it will be for such a client to allow a fellow Christian counsellor to support him through definite stress periods. Later this Christian client should be able to transfer his need for support to others in the Church.

Many more counsellors and ministers are concerned today about the total wholeness of the Church. Consequently more information and/or help is available to the Churches to maintain the emotional maturity of their members. As more accurate insights into human personality are given in the Churches, the use of defence mechanisms will be minimised, and the personality of the individual Christian will grow into maturity.

One fact which needs to be preached, is that emotions must be accepted *not* denied. In Christian Churches, feelings may often be negated or at the best labelled as untrustworthy. As a result, belief not love becomes the sole criterion for being a Christian (John 13:34-35). This denies the fact that emotions are always a valid and necessary aspect of experience. Thus, the client has a right to feel his emotions and should not be encouraged by some in the Church to repress them. Bereavement is often an example of this. It is unchristian (as well as unhealthy), to counsel the person not to grieve as this shows a lack of faith in eternal life. If a minister were to say at a funeral, "You must not cry now, just think about your mother being with the Lord" — this promotes a denial of feelings. It will even produce another feeling — guilt — which then must be repressed. The Christian needs to be reminded from scripture to accept a wide range of feelings and so to be able to "rejoice with those who rejoice; mourn with those who mourn" (Romans 12:15).

Another principle needs to be preached more in Christian fellowships to counteract the reliance on defence mechanisms. It is this: negative feelings can be recognised rather than repressed or sublimated. Pain, loneliness, failure, lustful thoughts, jealousy, hatred toward a brother, anger toward God, bitterness over suffering, envy over the spiritual gift of another Christian, or the hurt from a Christian who has deceived you — all these negative feelings can be acknowledged to oneself. Within a small supportive fellowship they may also be shared, if necessary confessed, and victory to control them can be achieved via prayer together.

The alternative may be a form of reaction formation. If the only 'allowed' emotional response is to praise the Lord as a Christian, then this praise will have to be extreme in order to cover up all the hurt beneath. But if the hurt is first recognised, then a conscious effort can be made to praise "even if you don't feel like it". This honest praise can become a healing for the hurt. Dishonest praise never heals, and cannot please the Lord either. "The Lord says: 'These people come near to me with their mouth and honour me with their lips, but their hearts are far from me' " (Isaiah 29:13). Even stronger is the warning in Psalm 66:17-18 where it says, "I cried out to him with my mouth; his praise was on my tongue. If I had cherished sin in my heart, the Lord would not have listened." Self-deception may be considered a sin, therefore it is necessary first to recognise a negative feeling and then learn to praise God honestly!

Points for Discussion

1   How may self-deception affect a person? How may the various forms of it contribute to (or cause) emotional problems?

2   What is a defence mechanism? Why are they used so often?
    Why is their purpose in alleviating anxiety rarely achieved?

3   How may a counsellor detect the working of repression in a client? What happens if the repression is never adequately shown to the client?

4   What is the difference between repression and denial? What are some common stress situations where denial is often used?

5 What is a 'scapegoat'? Why may a specific person be chosen for this role and what are the psychological consequences for the person used as a 'scapegoat'?

6 How may reaction formation be detected in a client? In what way may a Christian faith contribute to a self-distortion via reaction formation?

7 How may the use of projection increase marital conflicts? Why is paranoia so difficult to deal with in a client?

8 What are the usual consequences of using regression? How may such a defence mechanism be learned?

9 Why is sublimation one of the 'healthiest' defence mechanisms to use? Why may sublimation be particularly common in Christian clients?

10 How may intellectualisation lead to isolation? Why is it difficult to confront and convince a client that he/she is using intellectualisation?

11 Why should a Christian be able to use defence mechanisms less?
How may specific Christian doctrines (if distorted) increase the use of defence mechanisms?

PART III
Description of Types of Counselling

CHAPTER SEVEN

Crisis Intervention Counselling

THE ultimate aim of counselling is always to stand beside the client in distress. The client needs to be supported until he can see the situation with sufficient clarity to change it. But the more intense the stress, the more acute is the need for such support. Whenever the client feels his resources for coping with that stress are minimal, the degree of support needed will also be intensified. In such a case, a crisis has been reached which does not seek help — it demands it. At that point either help is obtained or the person succumbs to more serious problems. The self-esteem of the person is at stake, but the prevention of a neurosis or psychosis is the real goal. Thus, if intervention is successful it supports the person in the present crisis while also preventing future psychological problems.

Definition of Crisis Intervention

Various phrases are used to attempt to describe a psychological crisis: to be "at wits' end", to be "at the end of one's tether", to be "overwhelmed", to be "at the end of one's rope" — but they all convey the one message, "I need help now!" The intensity of the problem plus the helplessness felt by the person creates the crisis. If a psychological history of the person were available, there would be many examples in it of coping with difficult distress; but now something has gone wrong and all the person can focus on is his present failure to cope. This produces a state of panic. Emergency situations demand extreme solutions. Therefore the initial crisis situation may spawn additional minor crises due to the desperation experienced by the person. As the degree of desperation grows, there is always the possibility of imminent suicide. A more comprehensive definition of a crisis would be: a perceived threat to the self that is so acute that previous patterns of coping are now futile. The more the threat is seen to be directed to the core of the self, the greater the crisis. For example, if a man who defines his worth via his job becomes suddenly unemployed, it is a challenge to the core of his being. Or if an elderly parent loses via death an only daughter with whom she was living, how can her sense of self continue? Intervention by another person is essential in such crises. The 'strength' of another is needed to absorb some of the shock, to advise regarding immediate decisions, but, above all, to support the person until a new sense of self emerges that can cope again.

These crisis situations are very common. Daily problems are usually dealt with to some degree of satisfaction, producing a sense of psychological equilibrium — "I am coping". Then either a slow build up of repressed stress, or a sudden appearance of a new threat, places the person in a battle for his psychological survival. At this point he painfully admits — "I can't cope". This is the theory behind the crisis intervention research, and it has been primarily the work of Gerald Caplan and Erich Lindemann of the Community Mental Health Project in Cambridge, Massachusetts. Their interest is in the mental health of the community. They view an effective crisis intervention programme as crucial to the maintenance of that mental health. According to Caplan, the acute state of crisis is usually followed by a period of disorganisation and confusion that lasts about four to six weeks (Caplan, 1964). During that time the crisis has changed into a better or worse state for the continued health or sickness of the person. If counselling, of the crisis-intervention type, were available in this interim it could prevent much additional suffering.

In the acute state of the crisis there is one major factor which makes for successful counselling: the crisis client is open to receive any real help. This client's motives are the best to work with: there is usually no deliberate distortion of material, nor enjoyment of their misery. Crisis clients just want to see a way out of their distress. Hence their co-operation with the counsellor is good, and they are not likely to exaggerate symptoms only for sympathy. As a warning it must be stated here that other clients will play games with a counsellor, to get attention and/or sympathy. Such clients need long-term supportive counselling to gain insight into their unhealthy motives.

But a person in the midst of a real crisis will be motivated to listen, and to learn from his misery.

There are many types of crisis situations. However, remember it is how the situation is seen by the client that makes it a crisis. How the counsellor would interpret the severity of the stress from an objective viewpoint is irrelevant. For example, if a woman lives only to care for her dog, and that dog dies, then from her viewpoint she is in a crisis state.

More common examples of crisis situations are as follows: suicide, bereavement, recent unemployment, drug overdose, alcoholic abuse, amnesia, runaway teenager, lawsuits, battered child or battering parent, broken love affair, abortion, shoplifting spree, marital desertion, venereal disease, awareness of a terminal illness, jealousy over spouse's affair, school failure, rape, financial distress, and serious car accidents. This list could be longer if other disasters were added, like the crises that would come to a whole community due to floods, storms, power failures, earthquakes, famine, political revolution or war. A community or a nation can be in a crisis state, but the very public nature of the crisis hopefully precipitates public help of some kind. Rather it is the very personal tragedies of people that most of all need the personal concern of crisis intervention counselling.

The crisis situation itself can be put into four distinct phases according to Caplan (1964). First, as the situation becomes worse, the person tries to relieve his anxiety by applying the methods of coping that have worked in the past. A young wife may have controlled her husband's violence towards her by threatening to leave him — so now she will use a threatening approach again. Secondly, the old method will not work in this situation, thus leaving the person feeling bewildered. If this wife's threats have no effect, as the fighting continues so does her consternation. In the third phase, acute anxiety leads to looking for help from somewhere or someone. Desperation now characterises the wife who cannot stop the beatings, nor survive because of them. At this point a crisis has been reached. Counselling (from whatever source is available) will be heeded. The fourth phase occurs only if such counsel has failed to alleviate the distress. With the hope of external help gone, the person now enters into an extensive emotional breakdown (psychotic experience). These four steps in the person's attempt to cope with a crisis are not only predictable in each case, but also emphasise the urgent need for Christian counselling services to be available.

Why are there so few Christians involved in crisis counselling? In essence, it is because too few counsellors are trained to deal with crisis intervention problems. Some counsellors just do not want to because the risks are too high. The counsellor may also become overwhelmed with the crisis, and feel he cannot cope either. The crisis counsellor needs self-control as he deals with the confusing emotions in the client, plus adequate knowledge of the techniques of handling the stress situation. To say or do the 'wrong' thing can easily change the crisis into a disaster. It is like the emergency room of a large hospital where, to help the patient, more than just first aid is essential. Thus, there is a real need for competent training for crisis work. This must include an awareness of its limitations. But it also takes a particular personality structure in the crisis counsellor to be therapeutic. A good supportive counsellor may not be good in crisis work and vice versa.

A good crisis counsellor is one who is quick to respond to emergencies of all kinds, from the violence of a psychopathic killer to the vomiting of a drug abuser, and still remain concerned about the people involved. Under pressure he must keep calm. Directive counselling approaches must be used. The crisis counsellor must focus on the facts of the situation while still supporting the person emotionally. This is a difficult balance to achieve, especially in an emotionally explosive environment. Directive approaches are shown in both strong verbal reassurance ("I am sure that you did the right thing in leaving home"), and direct censure ("You may feel like really hurting him, but to do so is wrong!"). In an authoritative manner the crisis counsellor must act as a 'sponge', to soak up the salient facts and emotions and then present practical alternatives from that data. All this must be done under the pressures of time (help is needed now!), and emotion (volatile feelings keep erupting). So the counsellor must be able to assess the problem quickly, advise wisely about its consequences and assist the person until he/she can cope again. This all becomes easier if the counsellor can identify directly with the client. Even as a former alcoholic may often best evaluate a drink-related crisis, so a former depressive may best communicate with a suicidal client. This principle applies spiritually too; he who has been forgiven much by the Lord will be best able to encourage the client who is now in need of much love and forgiveness (Luke 7:47). A pride in one's spiritual state will prevent this identification with the client. The Christian must identify enough with the pain of the problem to be helpful. If, like the Pharisee, all the counsellor can do is to thank God he is *not* like the person (Luke 18:9-14), then he would also be better off *not* counselling.

Limitations of Crisis Counselling

Crisis intervention counselling is a short-term contact with a person or family in acute distress. During the emergency, much exposure of the client occurs as deep emotions are expressed — sometimes to the surprise of the client. But, after the emergency phase has ended, the client may be ashamed to return to the counsellor. Why? Because the counsellor has seen him as he is under stress. Perhaps this sense of shame, particularly in a Christian client, will motivate a quick termination of any further counselling relationship. The mask has slipped too far, so now this client must retreat and attempt to repair the damage alone — or with the help of another counsellor. Thus the original counsellor contacted should be aware that his own intense involvement with the client may be short-lived. It is always wise to assume that the present contact with the client may be the one and only counselling opportunity. Because of this, the ability to relate to another quickly and then to be able to release that person just as quickly — this is a prerequisite for crisis counselling.

Another limitation of crisis counselling is that some clients will *not* make it through the crisis. Suicide may occur, a denial of their Christian faith may be evident, or a life lived out in a mental institution may be the result. Whenever the outcome is negative, the counsellor confronts himself with the question, "In what way am I responsible for that person's death, denial or disease?" This confrontation can condemn the counsellor to a burden of unrealistic guilt. If the counsellor was far more reliant on himself than on God during the crisis intervention, then the guilt can lead to extreme self-condemnation. Or if the counsellor handled a crisis client without being prepared for the stress situation, or without someone with whom to discuss the person — then there may be guilt combined with real anger. This emotional combination produces in the counsellor a sense of failure, failure that leads to a withdrawal from any further crisis counselling.

In all of these cases, the problems can be prevented if only other, more competently trained counsellors are available to evaluate the stress situation with the counsellor. Support can be given only if it is also being received. Fears about dealing with specific crises are realistic. One counsellor may be shaken by the sight of a drunk and another counsellor may be ignorant about the warning signs of a crisis (e.g. when a suicide threat should be treated seriously), but each should be able to discuss these problems with a team of counsellors. Mutual support can be achieved only by this regular sharing, which prevents fears and ignorance from getting out of control.

These discussions with other counsellors help to keep the aim of crisis intervention in focus. The purpose is always symptom relief, to reduce the current anxiety of the client. More in-depth problems cannot be considered, and the counsellor should be aware of this limitation. No matter how much the counsellor may wish to probe into the causes of the problem, he cannot. The counsellor's 'ego' may want to prove his hypothesis about the client's personality, but he must realise that this is not possible. It is often obvious that a particular crisis will be sure to recur without some insight by the client into its causes. Yet this still is not a reason for reaching into the client's personal history of stress — the facts of the current dilemma alone must be dealt with. Perhaps if the imminent distress is lessened, then the client may take the step of seeking additional help, either from the same counsellor or from another. But this cannot be known at the time of the initial crisis. The counsellor's communication of real concern for the person in stress will help to strengthen this possibility for the future. Nevertheless, the frustration of incompleteness must always be accepted by the counsellor as a necessary consequence of crisis counselling.

Presentation of the Gospel within Counselling

In the gospel records of the life of Christ there is an interesting phenomenon: Christ taught truth and healed diseases but often quite independently of each other. Apparently because he knew what was in man's mind (John 6:64), there were times when he healed the sick without also teaching them some truth (Luke 7:12-17; Luke 4:39-41; Mark 8:22-26; Mark 7:31-37; Matthew 12:15), while at other times he used the healing as an opportunity for teaching (Luke 5:17-26; Mark 9:14-29; Mark 5:1-20; Matthew 15:22-25). When Jesus healed the man born blind (John 9:1-41), it caused a whole chain of consequences, in the man himself, his family, the Pharisees, and the disciples. In the midst of the controversy over this healing, Jesus went back to the man and explained how spiritual blindness is worse than physical blindness. It was then that the man was converted (John 9:38). The healing became part of the preparation for conversion.

For the Christian today, every act of service to attempt to meet the needs of another can prepare the person to receive God's love. It can range from feeding the hungry, to visiting the prisoners, to caring for the sick, but each act will receive its reward from the Lord (Matthew 25:34-40; 1 Corinthians 15:58). The key element in this service is always the motive. The motive should be love, and then it is done as if the person in need were Christ himself. Clearly such service does not just include a presentation of the gospel message, whether preached from a pulpit or shared between individuals. Anything which alleviates the hurts of a person may prepare that individual for the gospel message. Love in action is the visible 'proof' of the invisible reality of God. Often a crisis client simply cannot begin to believe that God could love him, if at that point no human being seems to care at all (James 2:14-17). But once practical examples of human love have been expressed by the counsellor, and received by the client, then the soil is prepared for the word (seed) of God's truth.

There is but one approach to follow in presenting the gospel within a counselling context. First, focus on the person's real need and try, with both love and wisdom, to help the painful situation. Second, after having earned the respect of the client in distress, share with him the source of your strength to reach out to his need. Remind the client, and yourself as counsellor, that your love is limited and your wisdom fallible. But because you have accepted God's love in Christ, there is now something real which can be shared with others. Go slow here. A full gospel message may be needed, or it may only antagonise the person who has been previously hurt by the so-called helpfulness of Christians. There is but one rule: to rely on the discernment of the Holy Spirit, and then to listen to the person and learn what his biases are before presenting the gospel. Try to begin with an area of mutual agreement, and then go on to build upon that common ground. Things to be avoided are: tangents into doctrinal issues, or condemning a particular sect within Christianity. But do not make your continued interest in the client contigent upon his acceptance of your Saviour. That would be an unfair situation for the client, certainly not an example of God's unconditional love for individuals. Yet out of fear that this is the only basis of your concern, a superficial commitment to Christ may emerge. This can lead the client into a short-lived spiritual high and a desperate crash downwards into the reality of non-change. This would create more problems for future contacts with witnessing Christians. It is easier to prevent this via a reliance on the Holy Spirit — who is the Agent of conversion (John 14:26).

Nevertheless, it is important to remember that an awareness of the client's spiritual state and a personal willingness to witness to the love of God in Christ must always be present during counselling. With these two factors in effect, the Holy Spirit must convict the client and control the counsellor — but all according to his timetable!

Steps in Crisis Counselling

Crisis intervention work moves fast. Therefore it is essential to know beforehand the steps to be followed for effective counselling. The basic therapeutic approach is always directive, not non-directive, which means the counsellor must know enough of what to do to maintain his/her authority throughout the session. What this involves is an application of basic crisis counselling procedure. The steps to be aware of are as follows:

(1) Listen selectively
(2) Focus on problem
(3) Predict future problems
(4) Confront coping methods
(5) Expect responses
(6) Contact other resources
(7) Arrange future contacts

Listening selectively means concentrating actively on the person in distress and filtering out all irrelevant and/or tangential statements in order to highlight the real issue. Other expressions of the client's anxiety (defence mechanisms) are ignored. Instead the focus is kept on the current crisis. Open-ended statements may be a starting point such as, "Tell me please what has upset you so!" From this answer, the counsellor must listen to the major theme and redirect the client away from minor issues. Via this listening process information, hopefully correct information, is gathered and stored in the mind of the counsellor to be used later in the same session.

Focussing on the problem presented by the client results from this *selective listening*. Only now more directive communication is needed. Often factual misunderstandings must be mentioned and clarified before the problem may be viewed without distortion. This means literally pointing out the factual errors in the thinking of the client whenever they are expressed. In addition, the counsellor must now interrupt the client to give short summaries of both the 'facts' of the problem and the 'feelings' of the client within that problem. The counsellor must communicate a feeling of his own, that of hope. The tone of voice as well as the words chosen by the counsellor can both express hope. Each client must be encouraged to expect a way out of his present agony.

Next the counsellor must *predict the future problems* coming from the client's present behaviour. Since stress produces a short-sightedness, the client cannot see where his present tactics will lead him. Thus, the objectivity of the counsellor must be transferred temporarily to the client to enable him to anticipate what is to happen. Sometimes this provides a challenge to the client to prove the counsellor's predictions wrong. But even if the client's behaviour changes just to spite the counsellor, at least some constructive change will be achieved. Again, the directive approach must be used throughout, as the counsellor applies a knowledge of human personality to the present distress of the client.

Next the counsellor must *confront the coping methods* of the client under stress. This will not involve enough depth to interpret defence mechanisms, but will simply point out how the client has responded to the current crisis. In order to do this, the counsellor must be familiar with such responses. Some examples of responses to stress are as follows: (1) to do nothing, and hope the crisis will pass; (2) to express distress in complaints and/or tears; (3) to release anger by words or actions against someone/something else; (4) to attempt to escape from the stress via excessive sleep, drugs, alcohol, sex; (5) to express the present trauma in a new symptom such as a phobia or compulsive (obsessive) rituals; (6) to transfer the trauma into a physical illness (psychosomatic disease) such as migraines, ulcers, colitis, asthma; (7) to cope with the current crisis via a reality-orientated approach, such as looking for a better job, or cutting off an unhealthy relationship, and (8) to utilise present resources such as savings and friends in order to minimise the misery. In this list of possible responses to stress, certainly the last two are to be encouraged as positive methods, while the first and fourth methods are always counter-productive for the client. Whatever methods are being used, they must be recognised by the counsellor, who then confronts the client with their effect on the client's ability to cope. If any constructive response is being used, it must be reinforced by the counsellor so that the client may learn other helpful reactions. When the client believes that he is already doing something right, he can go on to attempt something else that is suggested. Any realistic (not destructive) coping method can be presented to the client as a challenge.

This challenge should *expect a response* from the client. As a test of the client's desire for help, expect him to meet a concrete demand. This may include: to go to a specific hostel for the night and telephone the counsellor in the morning; to leave his medicine with the counsellor to avoid any overdose; to return to a parental home temporarily; or to surrender to the counsellor a weapon that was to be used in a revenge situation. Each act asked for must be within the capacity of the client to perform, and when it is done it shows that he/she is able to behave in a responsible manner. If the client profusely promises to meet this demand, but does not — then the prognosis for recovery from the crisis is poor. This 'responsibility testing' also enables the client to realise early in the counselling relationship that he must learn to cope by changing his behaviour.

In cases of severe stress, the counsellor must *contact outside resources*. With others involved, more help is available to the client. Perhaps the person's family should become involved, or legal and/or police authorities, or social service agencies and/or supportive Church groups could be contacted. This enlisting of others provides additional information and support to the counsellor too. With the exception of an imminent suicidal client, each case must have the approval of the client first before other resources are brought in. A willingness in the client to work through the issues with appropriate agencies is in itself a positive sign in crisis counselling. Obviously, the counsellor must have relevant knowledge of these agencies in the first place.

Finally, during the crisis counselling session some *arrangements* must be made regarding *future counselling contacts*. The counsellor's willingness to continue the involvement and a specific telephone number to call if the crisis gets worse — these must be communicated to the person. The next day, the client may see the crisis quite differently. Reactions like fear, shame, or complete despair may prevent the client from ever continuing a counselling relationship. Yet an opportunity for more help should always be there for the client, if he wants it. Further counselling may be essential. However, this must be left for the client to initiate as the counsellor remains available.

These seven steps should be used as guidelines, for the counsellor in the midst of the emotionally charged crisis. They provide a structure from which action may emerge out of chaos. They enable the counsellor to be hopeful as well as helpful as he/she directs the communication into these specific strategies. Once the fear of not knowing what to do next is lessened, the counsellor's concerns may be more properly channelled into being a vehicle for God's love to be communicated to the client.

Points for Discussion

1   What is the basic difference between Crisis Intervention counselling and Supportive Counselling? May one type of counselling merge into the other?

2   What is a psychological crisis? What are the usual behavioural symptoms of such a crisis? What are the goals of Crisis Intervention counselling?

3   How may a crisis situation develop, e.g. what are the four steps usually involved?

4   What are the necessary personality traits which should be found in a Crisis Intervention counsellor?

5   How may the short-lived contact between client and counsellor become a major counselling problem? How can the counsellor deal with his own sense of guilt after a crisis situation has degenerated into suicide, institutionalisation etc?

6   How may the Gospel be presented within a counselling context?

7   Review the specific steps in Crisis Intervention counselling. How may these points best be learned and then applied?

8   What is 'responsibility testing' as a method in Crisis Intervention counselling? In what way may it be used as a barometer of the expected outcome of the counselling itself?

9   How may outside sources of help be integrated within the counselling of crisis situations? Why is follow-up after crisis counselling essential?

CHAPTER EIGHT
Supportive Counselling

TIME is often referred to as the great healer. Whatever the problem, it is assumed that time will minimise its pain. Yet that psychic pain may simply go underground (be repressed), rather than be healed. This means that on the surface a person may appear to be coping, to have conquered past hurts, but there is a repressed chaos within. More and more effort is needed just to maintain this mask of mastery. Over time, this mask begins to slip. The person finds he can no longer run from himself. Physical symptoms (from insomnia to hypertension), plus a spiritual dullness may then combine to create even more confusion within.

At this point, the person knows he is trapped. Small problems are seen as momentous problems, and even simple tasks in the job environment are too complicated. Other people begin to respond to the person differently. There are some who misunderstand these distress signals and withdraw any emotional support; others may understand something of the stress and offer sympathy; and still others may simply become angry at the 'strong' person who is now acting 'weak'. Thus, for various reasons, relationships with others become so stressful that they are part of the problem rather than part of the solution. Therefore, the individual finds himself in a threefold dilemma:

(1) he cannot relate to and/or understand himself any more;

(2) he cannot relate to or expect support from other people, and

(3) he cannot cope with external and/or work-related pressures.

Over time these three signs of emotional distress combine, and hopefully the person realises that psychological help of some sort is mandatory.

Definition of Supportive Counselling

Although the problem has been made worse over time, time becomes one factor in the healing process as well. Even as the problem followed a certain pattern in its development, so now the treatment plan must follow a similar pattern. With one major exception (psychoses), the personality develops in the following sequence: relationships lead to reality which leads to reason. In this way, relationships with others structure the reality of the external environment; from this structure the mind develops its capacity to think or reason. Thus the source of rational and/or irrational thinking is the quality of the early relationships with people in the individual's life. (See Figure 6 below).

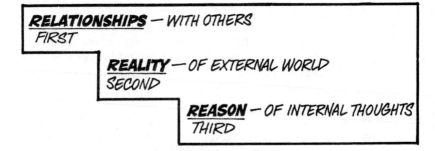

RELATIONSHIPS — *WITH OTHERS*
FIRST

    REALITY — *OF EXTERNAL WORLD*
    SECOND

        REASON — *OF INTERNAL THOUGHTS*
        THIRD

Fig. 6 : **THE NORMAL PATTERN OF PSYCHOLOGICAL GROWTH**

Early in childhood, even during the first weeks of life when the world' is a confusing wonder to the infant's senses, the most stable and significant element is a person — usually the mother or father. It is the consistency of their care for the infant that forms the foundation of the first relationship with another person. Can they be trusted to be there whenever the needs of the infant demand some attention? Through their actions the first sense of reality is communicated to that baby. Later, as he grows out of infancy, more of the rules of reality, the moral and physical order for his life, will most of all be learned from his parental relationship. In this way, a sense of reality (what is real and what can be expected) will develop out of a relationship of love and care. But if the initial parental relationship showed little consistent love or care, then the child will develop a confused sense of what reality is all about. Either way, it is from people close to him that reality is learned by the child. Patterns of reasoning within the child's mind are based upon his understanding of reality. Thoughts become internal expectations based on past external experiences firstly with people and secondly with things.

The major exception to this principle of development would be a psychotic personality. In psychoses the pattern is apparently reversed: reason leads to reality which forms the basis of any relationship. The starting point becomes the distortions within the mind. An austic child, a schizophrenic young adult or a senile senior citizen, is not able to reason correctly. Yet that person's irrationality determines what is picked up and distorted through the senses about external reality. Reality is seen as inconsistent and confusing. People, who are part of reality, are confusing too. In fact, such diseased states as psychoses make communication with others very difficult.

For most people the normal pattern of development is that relationships are the starting point for reality and reasoning. When this is so, a significant principle for counselling emerges. Relationships can *continue* to form the basis of reality from which reasoning can be altered. Thus change can still occur in the personality via relationships. Supportive counselling is essentially such a relationship. There is one related psychological principle: change can most easily occur when the person feels loved. To change one's view of self, others or the world always takes the courage to admit distortions and then to integrate the 'new' ideas into the 'old' personality. Within the security of the counselling relationship a genuine love for the client may develop which thus encourages change in his personality. But a great deal of time is necessary to establish a deep human relationship (a counsellor-client relationship), from which healing may occur for the client. Because of a long-term counselling relationship the client's assumptions about reality are challenged (corrected), and he is then able to use his ability to reason more accurately.

If change is the result of a relationship, then the Christian counsellor can initiate change in the client through two supportive relationships. The first is on a needed human level with the counsellor as a distinct person; while the second is on a divine level via contact with the Person of Christ. With two

ongoing and constructive relationships in process the possibilities for change are multiplied. Only a Christian counsellor
is able to encourage both relationships within a therapeutic
context. Insights about specific behaviours in need of correction
can come through the discussions with the counsellor and/or
through the communication with God in prayer.

There is a sense in which the human counsellor is always co-
operating with the divine Counsellor (Isaiah 50:4-5). As such he
must be careful to listen to what God is doing in that client's life,
and then proceed under the direction of the Holy Spirit. Supportive counselling, in the Christian sense, is the establishment
over time of *two* relationships of trust that become the catalyst
for constructive change in the client's personality.

Limitations of Supportive Counselling

It is impossible to work within a counselling process effectively
without knowing the limitations of the procedure. Once these
limitations are acknowledged for a particular client, then the
counseller can make either a referral or a termination of the case
without feeling guilty.

Limitations in supportive counselling revolve around the very
practical factors in the relationship. One of these is the counsellor's lack of sufficient training. He may be unable to know what
the real porblem is, or how to probe into the client's psyche
enough to get at it. The counsellor must be honest enough to
admit that a particular problem is out of his/her depth.
Ignorance of personality development, symptom substitutions,
defensive cover-ups, hereditary factors, family background,
repressed early memories, psychotic delusions, attention-
seeking motives, medication effects, or an unconfessed sin, can
all contribute to a state of stagnation in counselling. Whenever a
counsellor realises he is unaware of significant parts of the
client's problem, but does not know what to do to rectify his
ignorance — then a conference with another Christian counsellor is needed. If together the impasse still cannot be bridged,
then a referral to a professional psychologist or psychiatrist
should be considered. Sometimes an honest admission to the
client that a difficulty has developed will be helpful. This
admission may in itself motivate that client to reveal more of the
pieces to the problem so that it is solved. But the worst possible

thing to do would be for the counsellor to continue his self-deception by believing that the counselling is progressing well. In such a situation the counsellor would be ignorant of his own ignorance.

Another limitation of supportive counselling that originates in the counsellor, is the personality conflicts between client and counsellor. Some counsellors cannot relate therapeutically to specific clients. Perhaps a younger male counsellor may not be able to communicate understanding to an older woman client. Or a married counsellor, male or female, may be unable to empathise with the loneliness felt by a single person. Since constructive change emerges from a good counselling rapport, these personality factors in the counsellor and/or client may prevent the development of such a relationship. In such cases, it is wise to admit the problem, pray about it, and then consider a transfer of the client to another counsellor.

The most serious limitation of supportive counselling is that it cannot cope with the medical aspects of the problem, either past or present. All drugs and electric shock treatments have their inevitable side-effects. But because the counsellor lacks a medical orientation, these side-effects usually remain unknown. It is important to realise that medical and/or disease entities can be at work, to contribute to the problem. A psychosis may be developing, which needs medication to be controlled. Only then may counselling be effective. Or a depression may be so deep, that anti-depressants must be given. This will first change the chemical aspects of the depression in preparation for other types of treatment. This will always require a medical referral. Each counsellor should develop a relationship of mutual respect with one or more medical doctors, so that whenever necessary a particular client may be discussed. Working together as a supportive team can enable the counsellor to gain needed medical knowledge, and then this knowledge or awareness of insufficient knowledge can be helpful in counselling other clients in the future. Ideally, the medical doctor should be able to work with the counsellor, each contributing his own expertise for the common good of the client.

One other limitation in any counselling relationship is the variable of time. Deep human relationships always require time to develop. Time allows a testing of the trustworthiness of each person involved. Superficial openness between two people is not the same as an in-depth disclosure of the self to the counsellor. Self-disclosure takes time. Self-disclosure by the client is essential to the counselling process. Without it the relationship will lack the power to promote personality change in the client. The problem is that most good counsellors are very committed people, so that their time schedules are full. This may mean that the client cannot be counselled as frequently as the counsellor would like for the development of real self-disclosure. But the time available, even if inadequate, must still be used. Hopefully, there will be some depth of self-disclosure achieved nevertheless. For a competent counsellor there will always be too many potential clients. The disturbing fact is that there will always be more distraught clients demanding help than he/she has the strength to counsel effectively. It is a difficult decision whether to see fewer clients (thereby developing some relationships in sufficient depth to allow change to occur), or to counsel more clients (without knowing them intensely enough to facilitate deep changes). Each counsellor must admit that this problem must constantly be reviewed to see where the balance falls — to the many or to the few. The personality of the counsellor may tip the balance in one direction or another; some counsellors cannot sustain a deep relationship with too many clients over time without being threatened themselves by such a commitment. Whenever this is the case, the counsellor should recognise this limitation within his own personality and seek to establish more superficial counselling contacts. With a greater awareness of the counselling process, the counsellor's skill should develop. With a greater awareness of his strengths and limitations in counselling, the counsellor should be able to make more in-depth commitments to a client.

Steps in the Supportive Counselling Relationship

Preparation in counselling requires knowledge. Just wanting to help alleviate human suffering is not enough. In fact, without adequate knowledge of how to help, more trauma may be triggered off in the sufferer. Therefore, the actual method to be used in counselling must become part of the basic preparation of any Christian counsellor. Then once this method is learned, the individual counsellor may modify it according to the needs of a particular client. Guidelines provide the structure to give a sense of direction to the counsellor, and permit later evaluations of specific sessions.

STEP ONE: ASSESSMENT — TO EVALUATE THE PERSON AND THE PROBLEM

The beginning of counselling is like entering another country. Everything the counsellor sees is new (either beautiful or ugly), even the familiar language since the words of another person have unknown connotations. So too, the client, with his/her problem, comes as an unknown entity, full of contradictions and surprises, prone to distort situations and emotions, but desperately needing help. In this context, the first essential step is to evaluate the entire situation — person as well as problem. In order to do this the counsellor's role is to listen and learn; while the client's role is to express and expect help. Since counselling is a process between two persons, each must have a part to contribute to the relationship. This means that unless each is able to perform their respective part, the process is doomed to failure.

(1) *Identify the problem*

The counsellor must be the detective looking for clues, and storing them mentally until a picture forms of the actual (not distorted) situation. Listening is the primary technique, and involves a high degree of concentration on the following: (1) what the client is saying; (2) what the client is not saying, and (3) what the client is doing. First focus upon what the complaint(s) is that brought the person to the point of seeking help. This would be the verbal aspect to observe. But there are often large gaps (or unmentioned people) that must be in the situation. Why would a young husband complain about his current financial problems since unemployed, but never once mention his wife? In this case, what is *not* said may be more significant than what is said. Listening also involves the observation of the non-verbal communication of the client. In fact, more correct information may be obtained regarding the source of the client's anxiety by watching *when* his facial muscles tighten and/or his feet and hands twitch.

In addition to listening, the counsellor must learn to ask open-ended questions to encourage more facts and feelings to surface. Thus, it is far better to say, "Tell me how your marriage is going", rather than the closed question, "What do you and your wife argue over?" In listening to these answers, it is good to remember a principle of interpretation: the important thing is not what is experienced but the emotional reaction to that experience. According to this principle, focus needs to be put on the person's feelings and/or expectations not the actual act. Thus, if a person's aged parent suddenly dies, but this is seen by the client as a relief or blessing, his stress in the event will be minimal. The danger here is for the counsellor to use his own feelings/expectations as the criteria for how upset the client should feel in a particular stress situation. Just because at that point it would be distressing for the counsellor to be bereaved, does not mean that it is equally difficult for the client to experience this. To prevent this introspection in the counsellor, a useful question to ask the client (after he has described an event), is "How do you feel about that?", or "What did that experience mean to you?" Throughout this listening phase, the client is picking up the warmth and genuineness or coldness and hypocrisy of the counsellor. Communication is always a two-way process. If the counsellor is able to project an image of true caring for the client, this will create an atmosphere of security to allay the client's anxiety.

After some genuine support has been established, and general, open-ended questions have been asked, then the counsellor must ask three specific questions. First, what is the presenting problem? What is it that brought the client to seek help? This presenting problem is almost always the objective current distress, which is usually a symptom of another underlying problem (real problem or cause). But the counsellor must work with the obvious, and keep looking for the hidden causes. Thus, Jane may complain that her husband John drinks too much (presenting problem) but the real problem (discovered in phase two of the counselling) is Jane's hatred of her father, which is transferred to her husband. This then motivates John's withdrawal via alcohol. The second question to ask the client is, when did the presenting problem start? This gives the historical and/or emotional context to the problem, and often is the first clue as to its real meaning. Jane answers this question by saying, "John started to drink during the time my father was so sick and died two years ago." It is also helpful then to ask how Jane handled or coped with the drinking behaviour for two years. This gives valuable information regarding the typical defences (defence mechanisms) used. The third specific question to ask the client is, "What made you seek help now?" If Jane's distress over John's drinking has been going on for two years, why has she come for counselling now? This will often be another clue as to the real nature of the stress in Jane. For example, her answer to this might be, "John's drinking has become worse ever since he lost his job three weeks ago — he is just plain lazy now, just like my Dad was!"

(2) *Understand the person*

Once the presenting problem has been identified and summarised so that the client is satisfied that his/her complaint has been understood, then the emphasis must shift to the person. This might be done by asking, "Now I have an idea of what is bothering you, but would like to learn something about you as a person, can you tell me a little about yourself?" It is necessary for the counsellor to see the person with his distinct characteristics, strengths, weaknesses, motives, defences and distortions.

For the problems, both presenting and real, can be dealt with only as the client corrects his view of reality. In essence, it is the person not the problem that must change. However, the method of change through the counselling relationship must work through the unique personality of the client. A verbal client, prone perhaps to intellectualisation as a defence, may change only as he allows feelings to become as real as thoughts; while a moody (hysterical) client who screams constantly, may best change as she learns to accept the validity of rational thinking over emotions. As the counsellor assesses the strengths and weaknesses (areas of balance and imbalance), one aspect to consider is the degree of rationality in the thinking of the client. Is he aware of difficulties that do exist? Is the client imagining problems (delusional thinking)? Is the client ignoring issues (repression and/or denial as a defence)?

One way of testing for rational thinking would be to present a hypothetical and unrelated problem to the client and ask how he would attempt to solve it. If an answer like, "I would do what the 'voices' were saying to me then" — a psychotic state of irrationality and delusion is present. Another client might respond to this same question by stating, "I would wait and just pray about it" — this may be indicative of the defence mechanism of repression. These answers become further clues in unravelling the mystery of the client's personality, which is the point of reference for all further probing. Thus, the more aware the counsellor is of the hidden dynamics of the client's personality, the more accurately he can counsel the person toward health.

Another aspect of the person which the counsellor needs an awareness of is the client's spiritual state. Is he a Christian? If so, what areas of strength or difficulty are coming from this relationship? Will this client be receptive to, and convicted by, the presentation of biblical truths? Or is this client antagonistic to anything Christian, feeling anger, perhaps, because of a restrictive Christian upbringing? This spiritual dimension will always be at work in the client, either promoting health if positive, or preventing health if negative. Therefore, the counsellor must be aware of this 'second' relationship within the counselling process as a resource for good or ill.

It is also important for the client to be able to describe himself independently of the problem. When a problem is complex and consuming, the person often cannot 'see' himself as separate from it. But when this client is able to step away from the issues enough to be more objective, this is always a good sign. If such objectivity is impossible for a particular client, no real progress toward health can be achieved until it is present. Ideally it should be present in the first stage of counselling, but in more disturbed clients (particularly psychotic ones), this self-objectivity may have to develop slowly over time.

(3) *Develop a plan for follow-up*

Supportive counselling requires the development of a 'new' relationship with the client over a period of time. But the client must be aware of the boundaries and benefits of that relationship. Some structure allows security to develop within the relationship.

This requires a plan for follow-up, a mutually agreed upon procedure whereby both the client and counsellor know what to expect of the other. The number of times to meet each week, the approximate content of the sessions, including specific areas that may be excluded, and the availability of the counsellor during emergency states in the client — all these must be discussed and a consensus reached. Sometimes this procedure is called a "counselling contract" and may even be presented in a written form to be signed by both parties. But usually it is a simple verbal agreement regarding the 'rules' of the counselling relationship. The important thing is that the client must be assured of where, when and to what purpose he/she is to continue to receive counselling. Also, some mention should be made of possible referrals if necessary, and of the confidentiality of all material discussed together. In this way, the client gains security in knowing what his responsibility will be in regaining health, and what the role of the counsellor will be in this same process. This follow up plan prevents the formation of false hopes (magical cures in two sessions). Also, as the plan is obeyed throughout the sessions, it provides a basis for the development of mutual trust between client and counsellor because each can follow the rules.

For any client, it is usually wise to support him at this point by saying, "You have taken the first step toward help in coming today, and that may have been difficult to do, but now let us take the next steps together and discover how much can be done to alleviate your problems. There may be even more difficulties ahead as we uncover some unpleasant things, but your life in God's sight is important, and so I think you are worth the struggle!"

STEP TWO: INTERPRET THE REAL PROBLEM TO THE PERSON

Evaluation via astute listening to the person may take some time, but once sufficient pieces to the puzzle appear, it is the counsellor's responsibility to put them together and come up with the real problem. Once this process starts, the second stage of counselling has begun: interpretation. There is a definite shift of emphasis for the counsellor from listening to confronting. This means that the counsellor must 'stop' learning about the client in order to allow the client to learn about himself.

This is the crucial step in any counselling relationship, where the real work of releasing the person from the problem is hopefully accomplished. Because of the mental work involved in knowing what method of interpretation to use when, it is also the time of highest tension within the relationship. A real battle is going on, and part, sometimes the larger part, of the client does not want to be released from the problem. Why? Because the problem has earned the security of familiarity, but emotional health emerges as a frightening unknown in the future. Adapting to the change in perspective of oneself that comes from wholeness often takes more courage than to continue with the current crisis.

There are two difficulties that must be recognised by the counsellor during this stage of interpretation. The first is that the interpretation of the client's problem may be wrong. As the pieces were put together, perhaps forced together irrationally, the picture that emerges of the client is just inaccurate. Conclusions have been jumped to from inaccurate inferences of the client's personality — and this can create even more problems in releasing the person from the real source of trauma. It is like giving the wrong medication for a specific disease, where the correction involves both the treatment of the side-effects of that medicine and the administration of the right medicine to treat the original problem. In order to avoid this danger during counselling, it is wise for the Christian counsellor to count on the discernment of the Holy Spirit in prayer for the client and during the counselling session itself. Also, some danger can be minimised by suggesting rather than emphatically stating an interpretation. This approach softens the impact and allows the client to accept the insight about himself gradually.

Secondly, the counsellor must be aware of the many diversionary tactics used by the person to avoid the real problem. It is correct to say that "you shall know the truth and the truth shall make you free" (John 8:32), but there are also many ways of denying the truth within the counselling context. The most commonly used by the client are simple verbal distractions. Whenever the interpretations of the real problem are accurate, but are creating too much anxiety in the client because of their accuracy, then the client will attempt to use a diversion.

Examples of such diversions include: anger ("You are insulting my intelligence by suggesting such a thing!"), silence (a long, low staring into space), avoidance ("It is getting warm in here, may I open the window?"), flattery ("For a Yankee you are not so stupid!"), or denial ("I am fine, that is not a problem that bothers me any more."). Any of these types of distractions should be acknowledged calmly by the counsellor, and then a quick return to the last interpretation should be made. If a particular type of distraction is used frequently, then it becomes the subject of an interpretation (confrontation) by stating, "Are you aware that every time the issue of your marriage comes up, you suddenly become warm and want the window open?" By thus discussing the diversions together, they can be controlled, even used as an indication of the areas of real pain that need to be healed.

(1) *What to interpret*

In essence, the purpose of interpretation in counselling is to reveal to the client the nature of the real problem. To do this some further exploration of his/her personality is necessary to confirm to the counsellor what the real problem actually is. It may be helpful in this continuing quest to hypothesise the *absence* of the presenting problem. This can be done by asking, "What would your life be like now if your husband stopped his drinking?" This question is a good test of the person's capacity to change and her awareness of what the underlying problems might be. If a particular client cannot see themselves apart from the presenting problem, there is either martyrdom (the problem equals their main pleasure), or denial (perhaps a psychotic withdrawal) at work.

Often interpretations begin by making obvious the oblique anxiety reactions of the client. Essentially, the counsellor notes which statements made by the client are accompanied by strong feelings (shown in speech changes and bodily tension), or inappropriate emotions (laughing at something clearly sad). When this pattern of anxiety reactions is consistent in a certain area, then that is the subject to explore for more insights into the real problem. The co-operation of the client is essential here, as some may become so defensive and/or self-conscious, that further probing is impossible. If this occurs, it is wise to focus the interpretations in a different area, while the counsellor still records subjectively areas of anxiety to come back to in another manner.

Other areas in need of interpretation include the person's distortions of reality via specific defence mechanisms. If one client

constantly intellectualises, another projects the blame on others
for the problem, and still another releases the tension in sublimation — each method of coping must be made known to the
client. Self-knowledge is always a prerequisite for constructive
change. The premises for action (ideas about self and reality)
used by the client must also be pointed out for the development
of self-knowledge. A client may express guilt, even intense guilt,
whenever a reference is made to any pleasurable activity. If so,
then it is necessary to confront this client by saying, "It seems
that you do not allow yourself to enjoy anything." A reaction of
surprise and/or anger may result, but if the counsellor is seen as
someone to be trusted, then these insights will be more readily
accepted as valid.

In summary, the counsellor should be able to observe and
then interpret anything in the client that is irrational, anxiety-
producing, exaggerated, self-defeating, or a withdrawal reaction. Because of the supportive counselling relationship, the
client gains strength to put into practice these new insights
about himself. Through discussion with the counsellor, the person can express verbally, and then behaviourally, the consequences of these new patterns of thinking. In this way, the 'old'
premise and/or reaction may be unlearned and the 'new'
thinking pattern is reinforced over time. Repetition is always
part of learning, so whenever the client slips back into an
unhealthy way of thinking, a reminder and/or encouragement
from the counsellor is needed to revert again to the healthy pattern.

(2) When to interpret

So much of effective counselling is a matter of timing. A needed
insight can be given too soon, and cause only antagonism rather
than change in the client; or an obvious interpretation can be
granted too late, after a client has given up any hope of constructive change. Discernment from the Holy Spirit certainly
applies in the area of timing.

In addition, certain principles regarding when to interpret
combine this discernment with knowledge. First, it is best to
give insights when there is a good rapport evidenced between
client and counsellor. In an atmosphere of acceptance and hope
it is easier to ackowledge an area of weakness or admit a past

failure that needs to be confessed. But in this context it is also easier to reinterpret that weakness and/or failure in the light of the counsellor's reaction to it. Often this will mean that whenever the client comes to a particular session with repressed anger toward the counsellor it is better first to explore this problem and get rid of it before direct confrontations can be accepted.

A second principle is that interpretations should be stated when the person has been prepared to receive this new self-insight. It is impolite and dangerous suddenly to suggest to a client, "You have a need to feel ugly so that others will have a reason to reject you!" Discussions about feeling rejected, the hurt of being isolated, and then the possible reasons for rejection should be had first with the client. Then each 'reason' for rejection may be eliminated in turn until the counsellor says, "Could it be that your belief that you are ugly keeps you from allowing others to get too close, and then you feel rejected by them?" By prefacing the interpretation with a phrase like "I wonder if you are...", or "Is it possible that you are...", the insight is perceived as less threatening for the client. If the new insight produces an emotional reaction of self-condemnation ("I am just a rotten person, who will never be able to receive love"), it is necessary to allow the client to express these negative feelings first and then for the counsellor to ask, "Would you like to get rid of these feelings?" If the answer is yes, the counsellor should go on to explain how 'rotten' or unworthy each person is, including himself, but that God loves us anyway! As the Holy Spirit leads, this might be a good time for prayer together, to confess and let go of all those negatives preventing growth and to accept the reality of being loved by God at that very moment! There can be no rule here, because each client's spiritual state will be unique — but often an insight accepted can lead to prayer for specific release from that negative thinking and/or acting pattern.

Finally, interpretations to clients should be given only when there is evidence to substantiate them. The computer-like brain of the counsellor must be at work here to put together the seemingly unrelated pieces of the problem and come up with underlying reasons. Reminders of past statements and/or experiences of the client that would support the insight given may be necessary to help convince the client of the validity of this new idea. Confrontation within the supportive relationship ("speaking the truth in love") is what allows this evidence to generate change for the client.

STEP THREE: CO-ORDINATION — TO ENCOURAGE THE PERSON TO COPE

The termination of any close relationship can be traumatic. Yet counselling contacts must end sometime. If counselling never ended, it would prevent the independent development of both counsellor and client. The more supportive the situation, the more difficult it is to stop the sessions. But it is also more imperative that they do end before the client develops a strong dependency relationship to the counsellor. If this were to occur, then the client would be able to function in the future only when the counsellor's support was available. Then it is the counsellor who is guilty of allowing the supportive relationship to develop into a 'smothering' of the client's freedom as a person. Thus, fostering dependency on another person is never an aim of Christian counselling. Rather an interdependence is sought where the person has learned enough about himself in counselling to continue to lean on others for support and allow them to lean on him in return. Ideally, this should be accomplished within the fellowship of the local Church, where both criticisms (as needed correction) and praise (as needed encouragement) can be mutually given to each member of the body of Christ. In this way the Church can learn to weep and/or worship together (Romans 12:15).

(1) *Duration of counselling*

How long should a supportive counselling relationship last? This question cannot be answered in terms of time but must be based upon the degree of healthy development in the clients. Can they now accept themselves, with specific potentials and problems, primarily as individuals responsible to God for their actions? Has the client been able to see that as he changes in attitude toward a situation and/or person, it will encourage (but will not guarantee) a corresponding change in the attitude of others? What specific new insights about frustrated strengths and/or feared weaknesses has the client accepted and applied in his behaviour? Are there forms of self-deception formerly used but now avoided by the client? Can he evaluate his behaviour more objectively? What areas of spiritual growth are evident? Is the client now willing to submit to the Lord for continued strength to cope with future problems? These are the issues that form the criteria upon which a realistic decision may be made by the counsellor regarding termination.

The goals of counselling are: (1) symptom relief; (2) behaviour change; and (3) self-insight. Certainly any consideration of terminating counselling must first ascertain how much, if any, progress has been made toward realising these specific goals. There should at the very least be some change in the presenting problem (symptom relief), and an awareness in the client that other problems are present (real problem). If some confrontation of cause and effect relationships has been effected, then there is the possibility of constructive behaviour changes as well.

Since change generates more change, this is sometimes enough to perpetuate the therapeutic aspects of the counselling beyond the actual time boundaries of the relationship. If via the client's imagination he has learned to project himself into a healthier situation, first in fantasy and then in fact, this can promote needed behavioural change. Or if there has been a healing of a repressed memory and/or fear, this emotional release should be repeated in changes in behaviour too. After a longer period of supportive counselling, over months and even years, it is reasonable to expect genuine changes in self-insight for any client. They should be able to know themselves and accept what is known without distortion, because first they have been known and fully accepted by both the counsellor and the Lord. But due to the longer duration of such a relationship, it will be even more difficult to terminate the counselling.

(2) *Personalities of counsellor and client*

Since supportive counselling is essentially a relationship between two people, the respective personalities of each are bound to influence its effectiveness. Either person may produce more difficulties to be dealt with because of his own motives for the development of the relationship.

If the counsellor is immature in his own personality, he may find it frustrating to let go (emotionally) of the client. There may be some expressed or repressed guilt involved, "There must be more that I could do for the person"; or there may be an intense emotional and/or physical fatigue level which causes the counsellor to complain, "I just cannot take any more of this client's burdens, so it must end now"; or the counsellor may be on an unhealthy ego trip from which this Freudian slip emerges, "I cannot let go of this client for I need him too much!" None of these motives is necessarily known consciously to the counsellor, yet each will contribute to more problems than usual in the ending of counselling. It is good, therefore, for the counsellor to examine what his motives might be, and then correct them by the power of the Holy Spirit within.

The client's personality weaknesses likewise contribute to the problems of the termination. There may be a real child-like trust in the counsellor that will not release the person to cope independently of this new-found 'parent'. In such a situation the client fights any mention of stopping the counselling and he/she may even develop acute 'new' problems in order to perpetuate the relationship. The reverse personality problem may also be present: the client may have such an independent streak that he cannot submit to the suggestions of the counsellor. A spirit of rebellion may be so strong that the client does the opposite of the advice given and blames the counsellor for the continued problems. Such a client would want to end the counselling relationship as soon and as dramatically as possible.

(3) Practical factors in termination

Some aspects of the counselling process may alter suddenly. Sickness, death, geographical moving, change in job commitment, etc, in either counsellor or client can affect the counselling, as can weather conditions and national disasters. These uncontrollable changes may terminate a counselling relationship long before it should be ended. Yet this is another example of how trust must work: if the counselling is abruptly and dangerously terminated, then the Christian counsellor must trust in the Lord to allow the pieces of the relationship to be put togther at another time and place for the ultimate good of the client.

(4) *How to terminate counselling effectively*

The counsellor, when certain goals have been achieved in the counselling, must prepare the client for its termination. Communication of understanding continues, but its focus is now on the belief that the client is better and can therefore cope independently. Substantiation for this belief should be available. The counsellor should be able to give examples of how the client is currently responding to stress and coping. Then the insights gained from the counselling should be integrated with these examples to encourage future growth. Specifically, the counsellor needs to remind the client of past problems which have been conquered, attitudes which have been altered and resources, like friends and job, which have been developed. These are all part of the preparation for ending counselling. A summary of areas that are still problems to be solved may be given orally or in a written form. Such a summary is often a help for the client to refer to after the relationship has ended. This will communicate a trust in the client who is now able, in the counsellor's view, to work out problems on his/her own.

Throughout all of this preparation, the counsellor must allow the client to feel that the termination is not a rejection. The counsellor should remain available for future emergencies, or another counsellor should be known to the client for future contact. Other positive resources, like a caring Christian community, should be introduced to the client. A Church fellowship, where the client is accepted as a person with something to contribute to the whole group, is the most constructive place for the counselling relationship to end. The local Church involvement should allow the person to be willing to grow as a unique person — knowing that in many cases he can cope, but when necessary help is available from others. And because he feels loved, this help can both be given and received within the community of the Church.

Points for Discussion

1   What are the usual signs (external and internal) that a person is in need of supportive counselling? How may family members and concerned Christians be educated to pick up these signs correctly?

2   What is supportive counselling? How does the principle that 'relationships lead to reality which leads to reason' help to explain why change may occur within a supportive counselling context?

3   What are the major limitations of supportive counselling? How may these be recognised and best coped with?

4   What is the basic job of the counsellor in the first step of counselling — assessment? What happens later in counselling if this job is not done adequately?

5   Give some examples of open-ended questions to be used during the 'assessment' step of counselling. What are the advantages of using this type of question?

6   Why is it important to ascertain the client's own perspective of his/her problem, rather than to apply (via assumption) the counsellor's interpretation of the meaning of the problem?

7   What is the presenting problem and the real problem? How do the two interact with each other?

8   Why is objectivity toward the problem in the client a sign of a positive prognosis?

9   The real work of counselling is done via interpretations in step two. Defend this statement with examples of specific interpretations and the purpose of them as used by the counsellor.

10 Why may the client use diversionary methods during counselling? How may the counsellor best recognise these and deal with them?

11 How may a counsellor prepare a client for the confrontation (interpretation of the real problem)? What part does timing and evidence have in the interpretative process?

12 What are the dangers of terminating a supportive counselling relationship too soon? How may these dangers be minimised?

13 What criteria are there by which to evaluate the effectiveness of a counselling situation? Who should do this evaluation and for what purpose?

CHAPTER NINE
Basic Methods of Counselling

CONSTRUCTIVE self-insights in counselling involve either a change in feeling (emotions), or thinking (intellect), or choosing (will). Therefore interpretations must involve one of these channels of change. Many specific therapeutic techniques have evolved to produce healing in the psyche via a manipulation of the client's feeling, thinking or choosing capacities. Some of these are best left for a professional psychologist to use, but others can become part of the repertory of the Christian counsellor too. Once learned they may become the basic tools for treating respective clients.

FEELING CHANGES IN EMOTION	THINKING CHANGES IN INTELLECT	CHOOSING CHANGES IN WILL
HEALING OF MEMORIES	IMAGINATION	DELIBERATE ACTION
ROLE PLAYING	CONFRONTATION OF CAUSE AND EFFECT	SUBMISSIVE PRAYER
VICARIOUS EXPRESSION	IDENTIFICATION WITH ANOTHER	REHEARSE THE WORST

Fig. 7 : **BASIC METHODS FOR CONSTRUCTIVE CHANGE IN CHRISTIAN CLIENTS**

(1) Feeling — Changes in the emotions of the client

Emotions, to over-simplify, are sources of energy that can either be expressed or repressed. Most people in emotional distress find themselves trapped by feelings — often contradictory, but always chaotic. Consequently, such individuals either express their emotions excessively, repress their emotions repeatedly, or a little of both. But this same emotional channel can be used to create healing within the whole personality.

One method using emotions and applied most by Christian counsellors, is the *Healing of Memories*. Ruth Carter Stapleton has written most extensively on this subject (Stapleton, 1977). The technique is essentially Christian, since it is built upon the premise that the sovereignty of God includes his personal involvement in every activity and/or experience of the Christian — past or present or future. Therefore, any situation which was hurtful to the Christian was shared with Christ, and can be re-experienced with him to release or neutralise that hurt.

The procedure used in the Healing of Memories is quite simple. First the client is encouraged to relax, to close his/her eyes and concentrate on just breathing. Each breath is held for about 5 seconds, and when released the anxiety within is also released. Then the imagination of the client is used to visualise the actual presence of Christ, reaching out in love to touch the client. The client is encouraged to 'feel' Christ touching him. The focus remains on feelings, as the client is instructed to share what it feels like to have Christ there with him in love. Only after this feeling has been enjoyed for a few moments can another, this time negative, feeling be introduced. Now the hurtful memory, in vivid detail, is brought into focus in the client's thinking. The client is asked to re-live the experience, going through each painful part again. As the positive presence of Christ is still being experienced it wipes out (neutralises) the negative remembered experience. This releases the person from the hurt, which has been translated to Christ, and he is healed! Although thinking (especially imagination) is used in this method, its primary healing ability is via the power of God in an emotional release.

Two questions should be answered by a Christian counsellor before contemplating the use of this technique. Which type of client can benefit most from this approach? And which specific memory should be chosen to be healed?

The Healing of Memories in a particular client may be a dramatic success, while in another client a disastrous failure. In evaluating which client can be a candidate for this method two criteria apply: (1) the person must be able to visualise again and verbally express the emotional content of a memory; and (2) the person must be clearly within a normal/neurotic thinking state when the memory is re-lived. This means that a client who generally represses rather than expresses emotions will lack the capacity to recall the memory in sufficient detail. Such an individual unconsciously blocks out the pain of the memory, and perhaps out of conscious fear, is unable to visualise anything. To attempt a healing of memories with this type of client assures only frustration and failure. Likewise, the person who is in a psychotic state, with uncontrollable thoughts fading in and out of reality, should not be considered for this method. Self-awareness plus an awareness of the memory will each become blurred in a psychosis, so much so that the mind's ability to concentrate cannot be sustained long enough to neutralise the painful memory.

A counsellor must choose to work with a specific memory, but is it the right one, the source of the client's difficulties? The symptoms in the client must all point to an underlying theme, which was experienced in that memory. If a claustrophobic symptom pattern exists, and a memory (from age four) of "being locked in a small dark room and screaming for help" emerges — then this could be the childhood foundation for the fear. But it is important to be sure that this same fear was *not* present prior to the experience at age four. If the fear came before the memory, then healing the memory will not wipe out the fear. In such a case, it would be better to probe for an earlier memory with similar associations. If this is not possible, then some (not all) of the fear can be healed through this later memory.

Role Playing is another method which can release the person from an emotional prison. It encourages the expression of long repressed and hurtful feelings toward another person. A pretend situation is created, in which the person who caused the hurt is imagined to be present, or in which the counsellor himself/herself becomes that 'hated' other person. This sets the stage for acting out (expressing) emotions within the security of the counselling structure. Deeply buried feelings may erupt like a volcano, in vividness and vindictiveness. After these negative feelings are out in the open, it is often wise to combine this approach with a submissive prayer — to ask God's power to forgive that other person and to be forgiven in turn. One common variant of this role playing would be to release the emotions via written (not oral) means. Letters, in which the client writes out repressed hurts are a method of emotional release. These same letters should then be torn up as the client and counsellor pray together for release from the expressed anger, hurt or hatred.

Vicarious Expression of repressed emotion is still another way of releasing a client's inhibited feeling capacity. When a person is already feeling an intense emotional reaction, but cannot talk, scream, or cry it out — then the counsellor may step in and provide the words (images) which will convert the feeling into something more objective. The voice of the counsellor is used to express the feelings of the client. Emotionally the client is thus able to identify with the feelings expressed vicariously by the counsellor. And because the client now feels understood by another, it is possible to understand himself. The nameless fears are identified, the terrifying anxiety has been contained in a word — and this often releases the hurts and creates healing within. This approach assumes that the counsellor has enough empathy to express accurately the feelings locked up in the client's psyche. Like each of these methods, some counsellors can use it more effectively than others.

(2) Thinking — Changes in the intellect of the client

Thoughts are always precursors to action. It is the intellect which interprets (correctly or incorrectly) the experiences of the person to the person. Meaning is magnified by the emotional context of the thought, but it is the intellect which understands or misunderstands experience. Thus, it is often necessary to change via counselling the thinking pattern of the client from one of misunderstanding to one of understanding. Once a new and corrected perspective of the situation and/or the person is achieved, then action will change in accordance with this intellectual insight.

Imagination is one method by which this new insight may be accomplished. Essentially it is a constructive rather than a psychotic utilisation of fantasy. The client is asked to project himself/herself into a difficult situation and thereby think about themselves in a new perspective. What if you were ... what would it be like? When self-pity in regard to the present situation is preventing the client from growing in spite of certain difficulties, it is appropriate to encourage an imagined role comletely different. What would it be like to be fifty years old and have a fifty-five year old husband and two married children? This imagined role, if presented to a fifty year old spinster, may be the means of counteracting the power of self-pity by which she is trapped due to being a spinster. For if by this mental projection she can see the difficulties of coping with a marriage situation, then the undesired present state will no longer seem so intolerable. It is also a test of the reality orientation of the client. If she can perceive no possible problems in the imagined situation, then there is a limited degree of rational thinking. This is also a useful approach to help release a person caught up in the bondage of inferiority and/or failure. Then an imagined situation of success is painted for the client, and as he is able to begin to believe positively about himself, his capabilities are put into action. Certainly much has already been written about the power of positive thinking' or 'possibility thinking' as a means of gaining needed self-confidence and over-coming doubts. Belief in the possibility of change does help to actualise that change in behaviour.

Likewise the Scripture is clear in its encouragement of positive thinking. This kind of thinking sets a pattern for expecting more good gifts from God (Philippians 4:8). By imagining a specific change in circumstances, the power of belief is released to accomplish that very change. This approach can best be combined with a prayer of submission to the Lord, in order that the belief may be securely based upon God's purposes for that person.

Confrontation of a cause and effect relationship is another method using the intellect primarily. So often the emotional confusion an individual is in, is the consequence of his own actions; yet this person cannot understand his own responsibility for the problem. But with the more objective view of the counsellor, a clear cause and effect relationship may emerge. For example, a young mother may feel depressed and become violent toward her children — but only when she is over-tired first. This connection, if realised by the woman, could prevent the development of the depression. But as long as this cause is not realised she will continue to be trapped by the effect. Once the destructive causal relationship is revealed in the counselling process, then it is the responsibility of the person to control her behaviour in that area.

There are times when a particular client is so immersed in his own problem, that the only way to break into the psyche is through an *identification with another person*. The person's feeling capacity is so locked up within that he cannot even feel his own hurt. Perhaps pride is preventing any psychological awareness of wrong from surfacing, so a state of self-deception continues. In such a situation, the method of identifying with the problem of another person (for an adult) or of an animal (for a child) is therapeutic.

When King David in his pride took Bathsheba and killed her husband to do so, he was confronted with his problem through an indentification with a rich farmer exploiting a poor farmer. After realising the injustice involved in another situation, he then could face the same injustice in his own action (2 Samuel 12). The prophet Nathan challenged David indirectly and David was able to 'see' himself through the actions of another. Counsellors may confront their clients in the same way. Any aspect of behaviour may first be illustrated via another hypothetical or real situation, and then applied to the current problem of the client. For example, it is usually easier to understand how a neighbour's wife could both love and yet be annoyed with her ageing mother than to accept one's own feelings of ambivalence toward an adolescent daughter. This permits the person to see a truth objectively before it must be viewed subjectively. Such identification with another can correct wrong ideas as well as confronting the client's repressed irresponsibility.

(3) Choosing — Changes in the will of the client

Motives are the reasons behind specific actions. However, there can be many, even contradictory, motives for the same act. Each action must have some cause in the motivational state of the person. Thus, whenever an individual is in behavioural distress there is a related confusion of motives; the will of the person becomes involved in the distortion of the whole psyche. In this emotional distress, it is common for the client to complain, "I do not know why I did this!", or, "Something came over me and I could not stop doing that!" The will of the person, which should be the source of control for the mind, becomes out of control in itself. Thus the psyche, like a ship during a storm, is tossed around even more because the anchor (the will) is not available to help promote some stabilisation. In this context, the client will be very confused by his/her own actions, and consequently must find some direction and reassurance from the counsellor.

One method which may be used to communicate this reassurance is simply a form of *deliberate action*. The client must be encouraged by this psychological principle: when feelings are confused and/or absent, act first and then feelings will catch up with the action. This means that even when the person does not want to act (the will may be paralysed), cannot understand the purpose for acting (the intellect is confused), and certainly does not feel like acting (the emotions are absent), this is the precise time when appropriate action is essential. Apathy, as an emotional state, just produces more apathy and a withdrawal into nothingness. But if the person, under the direction of the counsellor, can choose to act in spite of this nothingness within, then the rest of the mind comes back into some sense of balance. The feelings will then substantiate the correctness of the behaviour.

For example, a Christian young man has just broken off an extra-marital affair. He has repented of this sin, but now has absolutely no feeling for his wife anymore. He may even complain of being somewhat hypocritical, having let go of one intense love object to be left with an aching nothingness toward another. In his confusion, he doubts his forgiveness by God and even considers leaving his wife. This action, he rationalises, would be consistent with his lack of feelings toward her. This situation suggests an application of the method of deliberate action. The counsellor encourages this husband to act towards his wife as if he loved her. This means he must deliberately think of her interests first, listen to her ideas, and be affectionate. This is an act of sheer willpower, but as this behaviour continues, he finds that his feelings begin to match his action. Now he genuinely loves his wife again. During the counselling process, it is as if temporarily the willpower of the counsellor reinforces the will of the client. There is a transfer of the counsellor's strength leading to appropriate action in the client.

This approach can best be combined with the method of *submissive prayer*. Whenever the willpower of the person is nonfunctioning, an admission of this fact in prayer is healthy. In fact, it prepares the way for the person really to submit with joy to the will of God. To realise that a loss of self-control has been reached, or that one's selfishness has perpetuated a particular problem, or that one has 'enjoyed' being self-righteous at the expense of another — all these situations require an act of submission and/or confession before God in prayer. Then, and only then, can a release come, to free the person from self and to form a new bond of love toward God.

There is but one important limitation in the use of prayer in counselling: do not force the client to submit to God. A 'willingness to be willing', to let go of the confusion within and to trust the Lord for the consequences, must be there in the client first. Then the counsellor and client can unite together to claim God's forgiveness (John 20:23, I John 1:9), God's power to change the person (Romans 12:1-2), and God's perspective to cope with the whole situation (Philippians 4:13). Of course, this assumes that the client is already a committed Christian. If he/she is not, then a prayer of confession of sin and acceptance of Christ as Saviour should be made before the emotional problem may be considered in prayer. The counsellor must first be sensitive to the client's actual spiritual state, and then to the power of prayer to change people.

The third basic counselling method which focuses on the will of the client is called *'rehearse the worst'*. It uses the imagination and the will of the person. In imagination the client fantasises the worst possible outcome of the present distress; with his will he then chooses what would be done in that horrible situation. The counsellor must maintain an atmosphere of support, otherwise the client's fears of the 'worst' become unbearable. The client describes the current dilemma in some detail, after which the counsellor asks what the worst possible outcome might then be. For example, if the Christian client chooses to select a divorce as the most difficult outcome to his present marital distress, then the counsellor asks, "How would you cope with being divorced?" This question forces the person to rehearse the potential feelings, misunderstandings and decisions necessary to try to cope with divorce as a Christian. This verbal rehearsal has its consequences. Either the client finds that: (1) the present situation is easier to cope with than this most undesirable alternative, therefore more effort (willpower) should be used to save the marriage; or (2) the possible future situation would be difficult but not impossible to cope with, so by comparison the present marital problems contain less fear of failure. This method makes the will work via imagination first, and often it allows the will to gain enough strength to choose wisely within the real situation. But it is the reality of the supportive relationship between counsellor and client that permits this hypothetical context to correct problems in the client. Scripturally, this method is found in 1 Samuel 25:26-31, where Abigail helps King David to 'rehearse the worst' in regard to the consequences of his planned revenge, reminding him that one such result would be to have on his conscience "the staggering burden of needless bloodshed". Because of this approach, David's planned violence was averted, and he dealt with the situation more responsibly.

However, there is one type of client with whom this technique of 'rehearse the worst' should never be used. This is the chronic worrier. If the client usually expects the worst in every situation (perhaps as an excuse for not being able to cope with the present realities), then to encourage more worrying will only feed his/her unhealthy habit. Therefore, with this type of person it is far better to avoid this technique and substitute other methods such as 'deliberate action' (in spite of worrying), or 'imagination' (to focus on positive possibilities).

Each of these nine counselling methods must be matched both to the personality and the problem of the client. If the person is strongly introverted (in personality), then the emotions are usually expressed less intensely, which means that the methods utilising emotions may be less successful. Likewise, if the problem is a fear (an emotional issue), then the feelings may engulf the individual, which makes the use of one of the emotional methods a good choice. Usually the principle to follow is this: first understand the real problem in the client and then choose the method or methods which will get at the issue through the same channel (feeling, thinking, choosing). Emotions can best correct emotions; thoughts can logically eliminate other thoughts, and decisions can override other choices. Since the real problem may have more than just one of these modalities involved (feeling, thinking, choosing), it will be necessary to employ more than one method. As the counselling process itself goes through changes (in either crisis intervention or supportive approaches), different techniques may be appropriate. But if the Christian counsellor is prepared via adequate knowledge of each method, then the Holy Spirit can give discernment regarding which technique to use when.

The wisdom of Proverbs 22:17-20 should be true of all Christian counsellors:

> Pay attention and listen to the sayings of the wise;
>   apply your heart to what I teach,
>   for it is pleasing when you keep them in your heart
>   and have all of them ready on your lips.
>
> So that your trust may be in the Lord,
>   I teach you today, even you.
>
> Have I not written thirty sayings for you
>   sayings of counsel and knowledge,
>   teaching you true and reliable words,
>   so that you can give sound answers
>   to him who sent you?

Points for Discussion

1   Why is it an advantage to the counsellor to know specific counselling techniques even if they are not used with a specific client?

2   What is the 'Healing of the Memories' technique? When may it best be used and when should it not be used in counselling?

3   What is the value of 'role playing' as a counselling method? Are there dangers inherent in its use?

4   What type of client may best be helped via the 'vicarious expression' of emotion technique?

5   'Imagination' as a counselling method may be very helpful or counterproductive. Explain how it can be used and its limitations with specific clients (especially psychotics).

6   How may a confrontation of a 'cause and effect' relationship at work in the client produce healing of the person?

7   The method of 'identification' may be used successfully with repressing clients and/or children. Why? Are there any limitations in the use of this method?

8   What psychological principle explains the effectiveness of the 'deliberate action' method in counselling?

9   For a Christian client, some use of 'submissive prayer' during counselling is essential. How may this method be misapplied to increase the client's problem?

10 What are the advantages and disadvantages of using the counselling method of 'rehearse the worst'?

PART IV:
Discernment of Specific
Counselling Problems

CHAPTER TEN
Distortions of the Emotions

EMOTIONS are necessary. Without them there could be neither joy nor pain. With them there can be either psychological health or disease. Often a synonym for any psychological problem would be an emotional disturbance.

Emotions are also a distinctly human aspect of personality, since they reflect the very nature of the Creator God. The Scripture gives many references of the emotional expressions of God himself. It also contains many examples of human beings whose lives have been distorted and/or fulfilled because of emotions. Perhaps the best example of this fact would be the book of Psalms, where the whole spectrum of feeling is exposed from joy (Psalm 16) to despair (Psalm 88), from love (Psalm 103) to hate (Psalm 69), and from trust (Psalm 23) to fear (Psalm 18).

Counselling involves dealing with people in emotional distress. It is imperative therefore that the counsellor know something of the types and symptoms of emotional problems. This involves far more than just knowing the names of specific emotional problems. Rather it should include some awareness of the underlying pathological process that led to the problem. Once this degree of understanding is achieved for specific emotional disturbances, then the counsellor knows what to expect in dealing with a specific client. In a sense, it is knowing which category to put the client into, and then being able to expect his/her behaviour to conform to the symptoms of that diagnostic label. However, this assumes sufficient awareness of both person and problem to make the initial labelling accurate. If the category chosen for the client is *not* correct, then the counselling process will be contaminated with a basic error — affecting the assessment and treatment of the person. Thus, accurate knowledge of specific emotional symptoms is essential for effective counselling.

Anxiety Reactions

The word 'anxiety' is difficult to define. It is an inner feeling of dread, a generalised state of tension, or a nameless fear of something. In small amounts it is not only healthy as a general motive for action, but unavoidable as new situations must be faced. In counselling, all anxiety cannot be eliminated. Rather the goal is to understand the source of anxiety and cope with its symptoms. Physiologically, anxiety is related to a fear response — with such symptoms as rapid heart beat, dry mouth, dizziness, frequency of urination, insomnia, and lack of appetite.

An 'anxiety reaction' is a specific emotional problem. It is a diagnostic label given to those whose anxiety level reaches intolerable degrees. It is a type of neurosis, which means the person can no longer cope with the pressures around his/her life. In neuroses, everything becomes too much to bear — even small problems may easily be distorted into large issues, and former strengths may be changed into weaknesses. The person believes he is doomed to fail, so he acts and feels inferior. This belief causes an actual crisis of not being able to cope. The neurotic becomes his own worst enemy, destined to repeat the mistakes of the past without knowing why. A neurotic is so trapped by feelings of inadequacy (both real and imagined) that he often reacts to others by saying "Don't bother me, I cannot cope". Thus, a neurotic is psychologically anxious and often this tension is translated into various physical ills as well. But the underlying neurotic core is always a sense of worthlessness. This produces the anxiety and inferiority feelings.

This gnawing sense of worthlessness keeps growing. But it is so uncomfortable to face such a feeling that it is usually repressed. At times it is distorted or covered up by many other emotions including exaggerated superiority feelings, and/or behaviour (running via activity). These avoidance techniques may indeed work for a while and thereby keep the anxiety level under control. However, as the months and years go by, more and more energy is needed to continue the cover-up. The repressed feeling of worthlessness becomes more difficult to deny. An anxiety-reaction neurotic may thus feel more and more superior (an emotional distortion), or appear more and more involved in things (a behavioural distortion). Physical fatigue and psychological anxiety increase and combine beneath the masks of emotional and behavioural control. Others are often convinced that the person is coping, even that he is emotionally mature. But the seething chaos continues within the person.

Soon the person realises that he cannot run from his feelings any longer. The repressed anxiety must come out somehow. It may come in a dramatic and dangerous outburst of emotion. This may take the form of uncontrollable weeping, screaming, head-banging, talking, or hitting of a thing or person, that lasts for a few hours to days. During this time the anxiety beneath the surface explodes in an irrational intensity — this is called an 'anxiety attack'. In the vernacular of the layman, this is usually referred to as a 'nervous breakdown'.

The term 'nervous breakdown' is an unfortunate one since the nerves do not break in any physiological sense. Rather the emotional cover-up is broken, leaving the individual exposed to himself and feeling very vulnerable. It is the psychological pain of honestly facing the anxiety within. During the 'anxiety attack' period, the intensity of truth about oneself may lead to many irrational behaviour patterns. The person may not just explode by screaming or weeping but may be violent or go into a panic state. If he is driving a car, the heart palpitations plus anxiety being experienced will necessitate either stopping or causing an accident. If he is in a room full of people at a social gathering, the anxiety experienced will usually result in running away or in acting in an incoherent manner. If he is undergoing a routine medical examination, as the anxiety level rises to panic proportions, the person may pull off the blood pressure cuff from the arm and run out of the doctor's surgery half-dressed and screaming. In each of these examples, it is evident that the anxiety neurotic reacts to normal situations in an abnormal manner. The anxiety takes over, as the usually calm exterior gives way to the chaotic interior and then irrational behaviour occurs.

An anxiety attack may last from a few hours to a few days. Irrationality is its dominant symptom. There may also be excessive physical strength to allow the person to open doors, climb out of windows, and/or break furniture in half. This irrationality may be manifested in violence, toward oneself or another person. Such irrational 'attacks' may recur several times, as the stress builds up again. As part of the panic reaction there is often the fear of 'going crazy', of losing a conscious grip on reality. When present, this fear intensifies the whole anxiety attack.

For all of these reasons it is imperative that a person going through an anxiety attack should never be left alone. The physical presence of another person is essential. Someone else who is able to share the experience can prevent the person from becoming violent as well as giving needed assurance about his fear of going insane. In the days immediately after the anxiety attack is over, the person often feels an intense guilt related to the 'stupidity' or 'harmfulness' of his behaviour. This guilt can best be dealt with by sharing these feelings with the person who was present during the attack.

Thus, the rule is: stay with the person during an anxiety attack, both to prevent violence and to reduce fears. But do not encourage the person to conceal (repress) feelings any more. While in the anxiety state, repression and all its falseness of emotion must get out. Only in this way can there be a complete release of the tensions within. If the emotional explosion is suddenly dammed up again, then like the water in a real dam it will just build up again to produce a flood at another time. Some people have periodic 'emotional explosions' that could have been prevented or minimised if counselling help were available during the acute anxiety attack stage. It is during this stage that another person (the counsellor) is essential to release more of the repressed emotion. Later in counselling these same feelings can be put into an objective perspective, so that the client may understand himself. Often the emotions expressed during an anxiety attack may take many months of counselling support to be acknowledged and then integrated into the client's corrected self-image. A corrected, more honest, view of self is the goal. Counselling can prevent a life style of a recurrent anxiety neurosis, by developing new areas of acceptable emotional expression.

Phobic Reactions

Whenever a 'normal' fear reaches irrational proportions, intense enough to paralyse a person, it can be a phobia. Any irrational or groundless fear that traps a person in its fierceness is a phobia. It is not a dislike of a certain object, but an intense debilitating fear that distorts the person and the situation. The diversity of the various types of phobias is seen in Figure 8 below:

NAME OF PHOBIA	DEFINITION OF THE PHOBIA
ACROPHOBIA	FEAR OF HEIGHTS
AGORAPHOBIA	FEAR OF OPEN PLACES
AQUAPHOBIA	FEAR OF WATER
CLAUSTROPHOBIA	FEAR OF CLOSED IN PLACES
CYNOPHOBIA	FEAR OF DOGS
MYSOPHOBIA	FEAR OF DIRT AND GERMS
PYROPHOBIA	FEAR OF FIRE
XENOPHOBIA	FEAR OF STRANGERS
ZOOPHOBIA	FEAR OF ANIMALS

Fig. 8 : **DEFINITIONS OF THE MAJOR PHOBIAS**

It is clear that the object of a phobia can be a thing, an animal, a person, a situation known or a situation only imagined. As long as the individual is able to avoid the phobic object/person/ situation, his life may seem quite within normal limits. But if that phobic person is suddenly exposed to the feared object, then a panic reaction results immediately. The point is that self-control is impossible in the presence of the phobic stimulus (feared object).

If 'claustrophobia' is taken as an example of the process inherent in all phobias, the following case study would apply:

A young executive in his thirties, named Tom, is working

hard to build up his corporate image. He is a university graduate. Tom has much determination to succeed in his chosen career. Behaviourally, he is responsible, a bit ruthless in business decisions, but shy in social situations. After five years with a particular company, he is transferred to another branch office to take over its management. The job is a promotion, and well within Tom's abilities, but it means riding on a lift to the twentieth floor where the 'new' office is located. Because of Tom's claustrophobia, if he were to enter a lift — panic would result. He might pull the emergency cord, assault other passengers, or even crawl out through the door in the roof on to the moving cables! In order to avoid this, Tom must arrive very early each morning, to allow time to walk up all twenty flights of stairs. At lunch time he must make excuses why he cannot leave the office, while at five p.m. (when all other employees have left), he must stay on working awhile and then sneak out and down the twenty flights alone. Tom is trapped by his fear. However, his manner of coping is easier (physically and psychologically) than learning to face the feared object.

When Tom's boss arrives unexpectedly to take him to lunch four months later, he tries to ride down with his boss on the lift. He panics and crawls out of the trap door. He is afraid this episode will mean the loss of his job. Tom's emotional problem has now been exposed, and his former coping methods seem futile indeed. But with appropriate counselling, this phobia could disappear.

What causes a phobia? There are two possible explanations of its origin. First, it can be considered as a learned response to a generalised fear experience. Thus, if a child is bitten by a black dog, the pain associated with this event will generalise to a phobia for dogs of any colour. It is also possible to learn a phobia vicariously. If a mother was bitten as a child by a dog, often talks about how dogs are vicious — then her child may develop a vicariously-learned fear of dogs. The child, in this case, identifies with the mother's painful experience. In either case, phobias are a learned anticipation of pain. But this fear of being hurt no longer stays within the context where it was learned. If this is how a phobia was learned, then what was learned may be unlearned. Counselling techniques can provide the means of unlearning — and the phobia will be gone. Some large mental health centres even have special phobia clinics to treat (via Behaviour Modification) phobic clients.

Secondly, a phobia may be a symbolic fear of something un-known. Thus, claustrophobia may in reality be a symbolic fear of death/burial. If this is so, then the real, not surface, fear must be exposed in counselling. This is done by probing into the events and emotions associated with the surface fear. The client's non-verbal reactions of anxiety to events, give evidence of the real fear. When it is known, the Christian counsellor can help the person face the reality of it. The various counselling techniques can then be applied for dealing with fears. A fear of death is universal, but through an experience of the eternal love of God in Christ it can be eradicated. A Christian counsellor may have the privilege of both revealing this fear to the client and then releasing the client from it via God's power at work. But to treat any client with a phobia, it is essential to determine first whether it came from a generalised learning situation or from a symbolic repressed fear. After its origin has been dis-cerned during the first stage of counselling, then appropriate treatment methods may be used during the second stage. One good question to ask a client to help in this discernment is, "What would happen if your fears were fulfilled?" In other words, what state would the client be in if, instead of avoiding the phobic object, it did overwhelm the person as it was faced? By imagining the inevitable consequences to the fear, the real issue is usually revealed. In the client's imagination it is first understood for what it is, and then the love of God can come into that life to conquer the real fear. "Perfect love casts out fear", but that fear must not be nameless nor symbolic.

Depression and Mania

> But I cry to You for help, O Lord;
>   in the morning my prayer comes before you.
> Why, O Lord, do you reject me
>   and hide your face from me?
> From my youth I have been afflicted
>   and close to death;
> I have suffered your terrors and am in despair.
> Your wrath has swept over me;
>   your terrors have destroyed me.

> All day long they surround me like a flood
>   they have completely engulfed me.
> You have taken my companions and
>   loved ones from me;
>   the darkness is my closest friend.   (Psalm 88:13-18)

To be without strength, alone in the midst of oneself, to be overwhelmed with feelings of anger and/or helplessness — this is the state of depression. It is a universal experience of mankind, known to earlier ages as melancholia. But in our own age, there is an epidemic of depressive ailments. These problems start with childhood depression, adolescent depression, young adult identity confusion, middle-age depression and finally end up with senile depression. Each individual at any chronological period will have mood swings. There may be hours, even days, when everything seems to go wrong because of a negative mood. But this is not depression. Depression is an extreme reaction of helplessness in which the emotions take over both the logic (intellect) and motives (will) of the person. The intellect of a depressive believes many lies, such as, "I am a worm and not a man" (Psalm 22:6a), "I am the only one left" (1 Kings 19:14), "Cursed be the day I was born!" (Jeremiah 20:14), and "Now, O Lord, take away my life, for it is better for me to die than to live." (Jonah 4:3). Likewise, the will of a depressive becomes paralysed, wanting to do basic things (getting out of bed in the morning, or eating the food on one's plate), but being totally unable to do them. All this is put together with a feeling of despair that never ends. In this way helplessness becomes hopelessness.

This 'helplessness — hopelessness' symptom pattern is basic to the forms of depression. However, while the helplessness feeling still predominates, the individual is motivated to seek relevant counselling help. But as soon as the hopelessness attitude takes over, the person often seeks suicide only. Thus, it is imperative to give the client some hope, that there will be an end to their misery — or else suicide will be imminent. It is also important to convey to the client the concept that during a depression their emotional reactions will be distorted. His feelings will be intense, but often very wrong. It is like a person with a high temperature, who feels warm even when the room is cold because his temperature regulator is out of balance. There-

fore, a depressive cannot trust his feelings, and so it is dangerous to use them as a reason for a specific action.

Anger is usually present in all depressions. Sometimes depression itself is defined simply as 'frozen anger'. This anger is a
heightened sense of having been hurt and/or used unjustly.
Often it leads to a guilty feeling if it is expressed. The client may
feel he is being disloyal to another or sinful before God to do so.
Consequently, to avoid this guilt, the anger is turned inside
(becomes repressed).

The object of the anger can be another person who has caused
the hurt whether real or imagined or even God himself. Somewhat like Jonah, the depressive may withdraw from the world
and just sit alone to sulk. He needs some word from God as to
why he has allowed the situation to develop in that hurtful way
(Jonah 4:1-11). But the focus of feelings is always on the self —
'my hurt, my aloneness, my rejection, my limitations, my
helplessness' etc. This focus is always distorted too, as the
emotions become the clouded lens through which all reality is
perceived and hence misinterpreted. It is easy for self-pity and
bitterness to develop within this context. The pre-occupation
with self can become an obsession. The depressive feels that no-
one else has ever experienced such deep despair and thus is even
more alone, without anyone else to understand his personal
plight. This is the paradox of depression: interpersonal relationships are found to be too demanding, yet the loneliness without
them is self-destroying. Because of this, the depressive is both
trapped within and isolated by his own emotions.

In addition to the presence of helplessness and anger, there
are other signs of depression which can vary in degree from one
person to another. Depression is a distinct disease. It will
eventually affect the total person in his behaviour, emotions,
physiology, and thinking processes. A list of these signs
(symptoms) of depression is given in Figure 9 (p.149). Not all of
these symptoms must be found in each depressive, but the more
that are evident the greater the depth of the depression (in either
intensity and/or duration over time).

Thus, not all depressions are identical. In addition to different
patterns of symptoms, there are essentially four distinct types
— each with a different cause and method of treatment. First,
there is *manic-depression*, which is an extreme mood swing
from elation (mania) to despair (depression). Using the analogy

of driving a car, one manic-depressive described herself by saying, "Sometimes I am in high, sometimes I am in low, and most often I am in neutral". During the high (manic) stage, the symptoms are excessive activity (to the point of eating and sleeping very little), and a feeling of omnipotence ("anything I want to do I can do and even excel at it"). This euphoria of experience may last several weeks to months. It will then convert suddenly into the exact opposite — despair. One day nothing is too big to cope with, and the very next day everything is too much to handle. This swing towards depression may last for weeks to months. In the despair phase the person will withdraw, feel excessively guilty and pathetically try to lean on someone else for emotional support. Next, normality returns as the neutral stage is reached, and this may last for years. Often the cycle of mania-depression returns again and again.

The cyclical pattern of manic-depression has always suggested an internal (psychiological) cause. Indeed, the research shows that this type of depression tends to run in families. It most often recurs not as a result of external stress factors but in a predictable time sequence. Every other springtime the mania may begin, or every January-February the depression may be manifested. The many months in between will all be within the normal and/or neutral range of emotions. Treatment of manic-depression is very successful when a certain chemical (lithium carbonate) is administered under proper medical supervision. The medical side-effects must be checked out. In some large cities, doctors specialise in this lithium therapy, and because of it the outcome (prognosis) for complete control (not cure) of the disease is excellent. However, many manic-depressives have to remain on this substance for many years — but the emotional mood swing is thereby regulated. Thus, whenever a Christian counsellor sees the behavioural evidence for manic-depression, it is necessary to consult with a medical doctor regarding the use of lithium therapy for that client. It may be also necessary to provide some supportive counselling as an adjunct to such medical therapy.

A second type of depression is called either an *exogenous* or *reactive depression*. It is a sudden feeling of despair as a reaction to an external stressful situation — the death of a loved one, an accident, a business failure, a divorce, etc. Normally it will last

SYMPTOM AREAS	SPECIFIC SYMPTOMS OF DEPRESSION
BEHAVIOUR	CRYING, BLANK EYES, THIN VOICE, NERVOUS LAUGH, SAD SMILE, WEAK HANDSHAKE, RESTLESSNESS
EMOTION	SADNESS, HELPLESSNESS — HOPELESSNESS, ANGER, GUILT, APATHY, BOREDOM, LONELINESS
PHYSIOLOGY	POOR APPETITE (ANOREXIA), INSOMNIA, POOR SEX DRIVE, CONSTIPATION, DRY MOUTH, FATIGUE
THINKING	IRRATIONALITY, NEGATIVE SELF-IMAGE, INDECISIVENESS, DELUSIONAL GUILT OVER MINOR THINGS, PESSIMISM

Fig. 9 : **SPECIFIC SYMPTOMS OF DEPRESSION**

between six and nine months. After this time it will disappear as the person learns to pick up the pieces of his/her life again into a new pattern. But during these months of agony, some counselling help is necessary. Suicide is always a possibility. Also evident will be crying, withdrawal and anger. Much loving yet firm support is needed, to confront the person with his irrational thoughts, while at the same time comforting the hurts and encouraging a responsible expression of anger. A depressive person can become very demanding. He may even threaten suicide if he does not receive sufficient attention via counselling. Thus, a balance between support and challenge must be maintained for maximum help to the individual with an exogenous depression.

The third type of depression is called *endogenous.* It is a slow, almost imperceptible build up of despair over many years. Finally, a climax is reached where something helpful must be done for the person. It is based upon an internal (physiological) change in the person and may include some genetic factors. Because the development of the depression is very undramatic, it often means that the symptoms are not severe enough to warrant concern from family and friends. Yet the individual is suffering in silence. In fact, because of the seeming neglect of others toward him, there may be even more of a risk of suicide.

Also, the absence of some external tragedy (as in exogenous depression) means that the person has no reason for legitimately receiving the support of others — yet he needs such support desperately. Without something specific to blame one's despair on, it becomes more difficult to admit it is there at all. Endogenous depression can continue for years as an unnamed and isolating personal problem. When counselling help is finally given, it can be a relief to share the despair. The client can also be helped just to realise that others have also suffered with it. The major feelings of anger and helplessness must be expressed and often anti-depressant drugs (from a medical consultation) can help to regulate this type of depression too. But through counselling both the individual as well as his family can learn to cope with the feelings of despair. Since it is a chronic problem that never disappears completely, the person will need periodic times of encouragement and confrontation.

The fourth and last type of depression is a *spiritual depression.* Martyn Lloyd-Jones has written most on this subject (Lloyd-Jones, 1965). He has shown how a relationship out of fellowship with the Lord and/or an act of disobedience to the Lord, can produce a depression. The symptoms are much the same as the other types, but since the source is spiritual so must the treatment be spiritual. With the probing of a Christian counsellor the area(s) of disobedience may be first discerned, and then confessed to God. As the reality of forgiveness is appropriated by the Christian client, his renewed acceptance by God allows a release of the angry helpless feelings within. Confession leads to healing. This process of healing begins in the spirit and then generalises to the other areas of personality. Only a Christian counsellor will be able to identify and deal with this type of depression.

Although there are these four distinct types of depression, it is still possible to have more than one type simultaneously. Especially the spiritual depression may combine with one of the others, or an external stress situation may aggravate an endogenous depressive process. The essential principle to remember is: the source of the depression will determine the method of treatment.

When Christian counselling is the appropriate method of treatment, two general rules apply. First, listen to the client's complaints. Draw out his feelings. This means the counsellor must get at the repressed causes in feelings of self-pity, bitterness, anger. Help the client to view himself as the victim of an emotional overreaction, where his feelings must be put again into a realistic perspective. Do not tell the client how much better off he is than someone else, rather accept the fact that for him the problem is both unique and isolating. Second, confront the client with the difference between feelings and facts. Once learned, this distinction will make the person responsible for recognising and re-channelling his emotions. The more responsibility for one's action is taken the less the person can feel helpless in the situation. Responsibility thinking wipes out helplessness thinking. For example, the more a person realises that he may not have caused the current difficulty but he is still responsible for not making it worse — this will negate helplessness. The client must see that he is responsible for his thoughts. If he continues to believe that, "I am no good" (a lie)', then he will continue to act in stupid, depressing ways (cause-effect relationship). But the counselling setting should provide the needed security wherein negative emotions like anger, and lies about one's worth, can be recognised and then corrected. A depressive is running away from some emotions and exaggerating other feelings, but counselling can be a process of righting the emotional imbalance.

Points for Discussion

1 Why are emotions important in human personality? Hypothetically, what would life be like without this emotional dimension?

2   Why is it important for a Christian counsellor to know something of the types of emotional disorders?

3   What is an 'anxiety reaction'? Why is it commonly called a 'nervous breakdown'? What are the behavioural signs preceding an anxiety attack? What are the usual consequences of such an attack?

4   Define a phobia. How may a specific phobia be learned? Discuss the power of a phobia to limit behaviour via reference to the case study of Tom.

5   How is 'helplessness — hopelessness' process inherent in a depression? What part does repressed (frozen) anger have in the development of a depression? Why is it important to recognise which of these causes are involved in a specific client's depression?

6   What are the basic symptoms of depression? How may these issues be covered up by other types of behaviour?

7   Why is it important for the counsellor to identify which of the four types of depression is at work in a specific client? Which types may the Christian counsellor best treat?

8   What are the general counselling methods to be used when dealing with a depressive?

CHAPTER ELEVEN
Distortions of the Intellect

ALL experiences of oneself must be interpreted to oneself. This is the job of the intellect — to think about and explain experiences. For this reason, the intellect must be involved in all personal problems. Even if the source of the difficulty is the unbalanced emotional and/or volitional part of the personality, it is still the intellect which will mediate the meaning of this problem to the person. Then there are other psychological issues which have their source directly in maladaptive thinking patterns.

Whenever the intellect is the primary source of the problem, it must first be recognised by the counseller. Then sometime during the counselling process, the client must be confronted with his irrational thinking. More clients are aware of their difficulties when they come from either emotional disturbances or volitional inadequacies. But the intellect often 'blinds' the person so that he cannot see what is wrong. Many individuals like to believe that their thinking powers are immune to distortions. Therefore, they will argue most strongly against any suggestion of inaccurate thinking. For some, thoughts equal reality, and in a psychotic person especially, whenever their thoughts change in context so does external reality. But the degree of intellectual disturbance need not be this intense before distortions of thinking influence behaviour. Yet the subtleties of intellectual distortions must be seen first by the counsellor in order to understand the complexities of these overt symptoms. Once the maladaptive thinking patterns are confronted and corrected, the behavioural symptoms usually disappear automatically.

Irrational neurotic self-concepts

Neuroses are the most common of all psychological problems,

affecting as much as fifty per cent of the general population. This disease is one in which the person may come in and out of its symptoms during times of greater stress (acute neurosis) or develop a long-standing reaction to any stress (chronic neurosis). But in either case, one of the basic symptoms is an irrational self-concept. The neurotic views himself/herself as inadequate, inferior, unloved and unlovable — in essence, worthless. All activity of the neurotic is interpreted by the intellect to prove to the person that he/she is indeed worthless.

For example, the neurotic believes he is unlovable, so this may produce either shy and/or aggressive behaviours in a social context. If the person acts in a shy manner, because he withdraws from others, others tend to withdraw also and this is 'proof' that the person is unlovable. Likewise, if the person acts in a physically or verbally aggressive manner, others will withdraw out of fear — again providing 'proof' that the neurotic is unlovable. This cause and effect relationship between premise and 'proof' is never seen by the intellect of the neurotic. Rather the reactions of others are usually misinterpreted to substantiate this false premise of 'worthlessness'.

Sometimes neurotics will respond to this premise by an attempt to counteract it. This may mean they will give in excessively to themselves. There will be much self-indulgence in things and/or sensual experiences — but like that of a spoiled child, the neurotic's craving becomes insatiable. No matter how much they have, they cannot enjoy it. In order to compensate they must have even more. They jump on to the neurotic merry-go-round of wanting more and more things but enjoying themselves less and less. Or other neurotics will deprive themselves of basic good things in life, like adequate food, a good job, a promising marriage, a well-earned holiday — all because they cannot truly give to themselves. Thus, if one of these possibilities for self-development comes along, the neurotic will respond in such an inappropriate and/or stupid way as to ensure that the opportunity will pass on to another. Then he may also have the emotional 'luxury' of envying the other person who now has what he lost out on. The real issue in either situation is that the intellect will not allow them to really enjoy anything (since they are worthless!).

The neurotic's behaviour is repetitive and rigid, especially in interpersonal relationships. As such the person is doomed to perpetual problems in the very area where self-worth is usually established — via relationships with people. This is sometimes referred to as the 'neurotic paradox', where the person's attempts to relate to others are always done in such a way as to ensure a failure. Such a pattern of self-defeating behaviour is the product of the premise "I am worthless".

A case study may best illustrate this point:

John is a university student. He is about to fail many of his courses and is unable to maintain a relationship with a girl-friend — but in either case he does not know why. He is just twenty-one years of age, yet feels his life has always been a failure and always will be. John lives alone, on the edge of despair. Television is to him an obsession, and often distracts his impulses towards suicide. If it were not for the reality of God's love in his life, he would end what he calls the "meaning-less routines that go nowhere". John's battle with himself, to find something of meaning within, is fraught with many frustrations.

One of John's normal needs is to have a girl-friend. He will see an attractive girl at the Church young people's meeting, share with her in a group setting first and then, with much fear of being rejected, finally ask her out on a date. No expense is spared to make sure that this first date is as 'perfect' as possible. He carefully selects the right place to go, what to wear and just the perfect phrases of speech are rehearsed for his conversation. If the girl surprises him by going on a second date, then this is interpreted by his intellect as 'proof' that she now loves him. Based upon this premise, John starts responding to her as if there were deep mutual love. As a reaction to this premise, he expects her constantly to be available to him, understand him and support him. So if he is lonely and cannot sleep at 5 a.m., he will call her and expect encouragement! Later he will call back again to apologise profusely for bothering her so early in the morning. John will tell the girl how inconsiderate and worthless he is, but because of her love for him, his life now has meaning. This is guilt manipulation. The girl soon feels trapped into a relationship where she must support his self-worth by maintaining an increasingly demanding friendship. Finally, she cannot take any more, finds herself hating John for making her feel guilty and abruptly breaks the bond between them. This is devastating to John — proof positive that he is unlovable. If he gave her so much of himself and she still rejects him, then must he not be worthless?

This self-defeating pattern will be manifested in reactions to things too. John believes that he is inferior intellectually, so he always expects to have problems in passing his courses at college. Thus, he will come home from classes to a self-prepared meal of mostly sweets and sit for hours smoking (which he feels guilty about as a Christian) and watching television (which he admits is not enjoyable). Then, about midnight, while half awake, John will open a textbook. About 3 a.m. he will finally go to bed, feeling everything is futile. The next morning he will oversleep and miss his lectures (for which he is not prepared anyway). In all this misery, the intellect will not allow John to 'see' how his own actions are perpetuating these problems.

A neurotic self-concept of worthlessness may lead to an active thought life. By thinking, goals are at least achieved in fantasy. For John this was coupled with another neurotic symptom — hypochondria. Some months after the break-up with his girl-friend, he developed an excessive concern about his own physical health. Vague pains were alternately interpreted as a heart condition (which killed his father) or ulcers (which his mother had previously). John sought confirmation for these fears from several doctors until he settled on a treatment programme prescribed by a sympathetic young female doctor. Each time John would go for a treatment and/or test, he would convince himself that the doctor was so gentle with him because she was falling in love with him. Then his fantasies took over and he would spend hours daydreaming about the doctor and thinking of ways to see her more often. In order to validate his taking of her professional time, other physical pains and problems soon developed. Each new ailment required more tests. Hence there were more opportunities both to worry about himself and day-dream about the doctor. This non-productive thought-cycle continued until an anxiety attack necessitated hospitalisation and psychiatric treatment. After release from the hospital, Christian counselling services were made available to John, who then began the long quest of finding his self-worth.

From this case study, it is clear that such diverse symptoms as anxiety, hypochondria, day-dreaming, depression, aggressiveness, insomnia, guilt, fear, obsessiveness, academic-failure, loneliness, manipulativeness and perfectionism — can all be the consequences of an irrational self-concept. If a neurotic believes he is unlovable, he will offend enough people to prove it. Then he really must accept his worthlessness, and will treat himself with contempt. The intellectual premise (self concept) produces the problems (in behaviour). Unless the counsellor is able to identify the irrational thought processes, much time will be wasted in dealing with behavioural symptoms only.

Delusions in Schizophrenia

It is during adolescence and young adulthood, that a serious type of psychological problem is most likely to occur — schizophrenia. Externally the young person seems separated from (unaware of) the environment and looks out at the world through eyes that appear vacant. Like any psychological problem, there are degrees of severity in schizophrenia. The most disturbed type will probably receive psychiatric care for much of his lifetime; but the milder type can and should be incorporated into the mainstream of society. It is a form of psychosis, which means that the person is out of touch with reality and has substituted his own thoughts and/or fantasies for reality. In layman's terms, to be psychotic is to be crazy; in legal terms, to be psychotic is to be insane.

Schizophrenia literally means a split (schizo) mind (phren). But it is a mind split from within, where the will, intellect and emotions become unrelated to each other in the personality. Thus, whatever the person is wanting is disconnected from what he/she is thinking, which is separate from what is being felt. For example, a schizophrenic may want to get out of bed (will), but be thinking about the strange pattern of colours in the wallpaper (intellect) while feeling like laughing (emotions). Each of these parts is pulling in different directions. This produces an inner state of chaos and irrational external behaviour. In this case, the person may sit up in bed, put his eye against the wallpaper and laugh uncontrollably. But it does not produce a split personality in the sense of a Dr. Jekyll and Mr. Hyde — where there are two intact but different personalities. In schizophrenia, there is always an incomplete or fragmented personality which corresponds to the chaotic split within.

The major symptom of this split in schizophrenia is the presence of delusional thinking. A delusion is simply an irrational belief, e.g. "the colour yellow is evil", "the electric wire brings me messages from Mars", "when I sit in that chair, everyone can read my mind" or "my husband is poisoning my food". Two principles regarding delusions must be kept in mind for effective counselling. First, although some of these delusional ideas are obviously wrong (irrational) to a sane person, to the schizophrenic they are right (logical). The thinking process is so distorted in the schizophrenic, that delusions are seen as valid. Since beliefs determine behaviour for everyone, if the beliefs are delusions, then the behaviour will be irrational too. But this very irrational behaviour will be understandable from the delusion. Thus, if you really believe that the colour yellow is evil, and scream and run away when presented with a yellow pill to swallow — this behaviour is consistent with the belief. The second principle is that sometimes the delusional idea could be correct. Perhaps the husband is attempting to poison his wife, or it is possible that one electronic wave pattern is picking up a radio frequency in a foreign language. Even if a specific idea is difficult to accept as valid, it is always wise to investigate the possibilities of its being correct before a delusion is assumed to be at work. Looking at the total picture of the personality will help in this discernment. When the individual seems relatively coherent, in touch with reality and then says, "My husband is poisoning me" and proceeds to give some evidence for the statement, it is more likely *not* to be a delusion. But even if the person is anxious, withdrawn and illogical, not all of his beliefs should be automatically labelled as delusions.

Why are delusions necessary to schizophrenics? Simply because they cannot face and/or interpret reality without a subjective delusional base. In a sense, the schizophrenic creates his own reality and then is isolated and/or trapped as a prisoner within it. As one client put it, "I am a king by creating in my mind anything I like: the only trouble is that my kingdom has no subjects." This 'kingdom' is always so secretive that no-one else can share it and usually no-one else is wanted. This is because thinking must have some common basis in reality to be communicated to another. For example, if two people cannot agree that today is Thursday, it is raining outside and a political election will be held next month, then how can they share different ideas related to political issues? For this reason, the schizophrenic usually withdraws more and more into his subjective (non-sharable) world. Delusional thinking patterns produce withdrawal and together they constitute the two major symptoms of schizophrenia.

A schizophrenic has certain types of delusions. The client may say, "You are not going to believe this. I hope it will not shock you, but my body is turning to wax." (Upon hearing this, one can understand the client's refusal to have her hair washed in warm water.) Or another client may share, quite anxiously, that "There are receptor cells (called 'azoids' by him) in my head which pick up messages from the Nazis left over in air vacuum." These are both delusions relating to irrational concepts about their body. Often the schizophrenic regards his/her body as alien, non-human and unable to communicate sensation accurately. They may be in pain, but not feel it; or dress inappropriately during cold weather, or even feel as if their body is the size of a small pea. All these somatic distortions probably stem from the discrepancies between delusion (thought) and feeling (emotions) in the personality.

Another common form for schizophrenic delusions to take relates to the concept of identity. The individual may believe that he is married to a famous television star, is an agent of Satan out to destroy the Church, or is Jesus Christ and has returned to save the world. This is a severe type of schizophrenia where the basic identity of one's name and family is counteracted by the stronger delusion of believing to be someone else. Like all schizophrenic delusions, they may be more intense at certain times and then almost disappear at other times. But usually when it is a delusion of identity, it is so obviously irrational that professional help is sought for the person.

A milder type of this same identity-delusion is an intense identification with (vicariously living through) the life and experiences of another. This is not exchanging one identity for another (believing self to be Christ) but a subtle merging of two separate identities into one. In this way, a borderline (milder) schizophrenic mother may lose herself via an absorption of her daughter's life. Whatever the daughter does, almost whatever she thinks, must be a part of the mother's experience. This produces an unhealthy dependency reaction. To such a mother, the daughter is literally an extension (or fulfilment) of her own identity. Without this intense identification, the self-concept of the mother is undefined (or too chaotic). The basic delusion here is that the mother believes that her daughter needs her so much that this closeness is necessary, when in reality it is this very intensity between them which will eventually destroy the daughter's unique personality. Perhaps it is the fear of not being able to interpret reality aright that motivates such a mother to use her daughter as a mediator toward reality. If the daughter allows this manipulation of her psyche to go on, then they both may end up more withdrawn, even psychotic, together.

Another delusional pattern in schizophrenia is the false belief of grandeur and/or persecution. Most often a schizophrenic with paranoid tendencies will believe in his own superior importance. This is called having a delusion of grandeur. These delusions make it necessary for those who resent this power to try to harm the person (delusions of persecution). If there is not a special ability and/or knowledge in the person, there would be no logical reason for being limited/hurt by another. For this reason, these two delusions (grandeur and persecution) are usually found together in a paranoid schizophrenic. Since paranoia implies basic mistrust of people, such a client is very difficult to work with in a counselling context. To confront a paranoid client with his delusions may only confirm his mistrust of the counsellor; while to agree with his delusions of grandeur/persecution may only accentuate them for the client. This is the dilemma of dealing with a paranoid schizophrenic — it can make referral to competent psychiatric personnel essential.

For many schizophrenics these different delusional patterns combine with unpredictable sensory distortions (hallucinations). The person may hear voices demanding that he/she do horrible things or giving them secret information about other people; or the individual may see images of people/places that are frightening and provide new reasons to react in bizarre ways. Less probable are hallucinations using the sense of touch (crawling things on the skin), or smell (a scent is detected as a harbinger of some disaster). But any one of these sensory distortions makes external reality even more unreliable and this encourages a withdrawal into fantasy (total delusional thinking). Fantasy becomes the only 'safe' or predictable place to be. The schizophrenic's delusions about self and the world provide the only tentative structure for his existence. Therefore, in counselling a development of specific strengths/resources within the personality must be done prior to a destruction of the delusional system. For this reason alone, schizophrenics are very difficult to treat and there should always be some consultation with a professional.

A disturbing question for a Christian counsellor is this: what is the relationship between schizophrenic delusions and the supernatural experiences of many Christians? Most Christians would admit that they have been given supernatural insight during prayer, that they have 'heard' the still, small voice of God to convict and/or encourage them, or that they have received a supernatural vision of what God could do in a situation. Did not God say that, "in the last days . . . I will pour out my Spirit on all people. Your sons and daughters will prophesy, your young men will see visions, your old men will dream dreams" (Acts 2:17).

Are these experiences simply hallucinations like the psychotic's? The answer is a definite no! But two criteria must be applied to be certain, since some Christians are also schizophenic and may therefore have both types of experiences. First, the Christian's supernatural sensations are always confirmed by the principles of scripture and/or the direct perceptions of other Christians. If the Christian receives an experience which is not so confirmed, he can pray for this validation. If it is from God, this will be done (Jeremiah 33:3). "I am the Lord, and there is no other. I have not spoken in secret from somewhere in a land of darkness; I have not said to Jacob's descendants 'Seek me in vain'. I, the Lord, speak the truth; I declare what is right" (Isaiah 45:18b-19). Second, the Christian's supernatural experiences must produce positive results in his life — the primary one being God's peace within (Isaiah 26:3; John 14:25-27). But if the particular experience perpetuates turmoil and/or doubt of God, it cannot be from God in the first place. Because there is such an interdependence between the spiritual and psychological aspects of personality, it is essential for the Christian counsellor to develop supernaturally some discernment of these interactions.

But the major difficulty in schizophrenia is an intellect which cannot perceive the falseness of its own belief and rarely allows correction of these beliefs from another. This inevitably leads the person into isolated existence where things, not people, are sought. Yet these difficulties in the intellect can be minimised.

They may best be controlled if there is a group (family, counsellors, Church community) which is willing to accept the schizophrenic and encourage his growth in interpersonal relationships. The more the schizophrenic does get involved with people, the more likely he/she is to take correction from others for the delusional thinking patterns.

Sociopathic Thinking Patterns

Perhaps the most difficult of all psychological problems to identify is that of the sociopath. It falls into the diagnostic category of a character disorder — which means a long-standing area of weakness within the personality. This weakness may be an uncontrollable behaviour pattern (drinking, gambling, overeating, etc.) or an underdeveloped ability (sexual, moral). A sociopath is simply a person who has a retarded (underdeveloped) moral sense. As a consequence, many sociopaths become law-breakers and end up as part of the prison population. This type of sociopath is outwardly aggressive, amoral and loyal only to others within the criminal subculture. But there is another type of sociopath where the individual is primarily charming, socially acceptable and may even have strong leadership qualities. In this type, the weakness is an inability to relate emotionally to others, covered up by an excessive verbal and/or intellectual camouflage.

Such a sociopath is often found in the leadership position of companies, countries and churches. It is far more common in males. The person possesses enough charisma to convince almost everyone of his leadership potential — and so to encourage others to trust in him. Charm, wit, social sensitivity and self-confidence are all shown in the sociopath's personality. But it is as if the words are right but they are 'sung to the wrong tune'. Although the capacity to charm is real, the character qualities behind this mask are superficial — even contradictory. Instead of being self-confident, the sociopath is fearful, and rather than being socially mature, the person is totally unable to relate to others on deep levels. But intellectual ploys are used to bolster up the weaknesses within, as the sociopath convinces others and himself of his superior social strengths.

Rationalisation and projection are two of the favourite methods used by the sociopath to promote this self-deception.

Activity, especially exciting activity, is sought by the sociopath as a rationalisation for not being able to feel deeply for people. He tells himself he is too busy to care. There is an absence of appropriate affect (emotion) in the sociopath; because of this, he would rather be distracted by an intellectual challenge than to be involved in an emotional commitment. For example, if his wife is dying in hospital, it is then that he would choose to finish a new sales proposal at the office in order to have an excuse (rationalisation) for not being with her at that time. The real issue is not that he does not care for his wife, but that because of an emotionally retarded psyche — he cannot care! Perhaps it will take the wife's death and his absence of any grief for this sociopath to stop long enough finally to realise that he has a psychological problem that needs to be helped.

Projection is the other common defence used excessively by the sociopath. He is never able sincerely to admit a wrong or accept culpability for an action. For example, he may say, "I could not do anything about the situation because you did not tell me to look into it." It is always someone else who is res-ponsible for what goes wrong while he alone is responsible for what goes right. This is because the sociopath cannot feel real guilt. He may feign guilt, even apologising profusely if this kind of verbal manipulation of another gains him some self-esteem in return. But although the words may say "I am sorry", the feeling of being guilty is not within his moral capacity. In this sense, he is amoral. Thus, the sociopath cannot really love another nor feel guilty for hurting another. (Love and guilt are always psychological correlates; if a person has a problem with one there will usually be difficulties with the other one too.)

An unusually active intellect is essential for the sociopath, since these rationalisations and/or projections are the only way his distorted psyche can try to maintain some balance within. The more intelligent the sociopath is, the longer these tech-niques will work — and the longer it will be before any psycho-logical help is sought. Even though his promises never equal his performances, the sociopath, like the politician, has enough charm to exonerate himself and get 'elected' again and again. In Christian circles, where forgiveness of a brother's faults is encouraged, the sociopath's problems may take even longer to be detected. But although another Christian may perceive the problem, nothing (except prayer) can be done to help the sociopath until he is aware himself of the need. Then a group of Christian counsellors, each confronting the client with his intellectual and behavioural evasions of commitments, will best be able to bring healing within.

The prophetic words of Isaiah 29:14 can be applied to the thinking processes of the sociopath:

> "Therefore once more I will astound these people with wonder upon wonder; the wisdom of the wise will perish, the intelligence of the intelligent will vanish."

Points for Discussion

1   Why is the intellect often the source of a psychological poblem yet it is so difficult for the client to accept this as the source?

2   What is a neurosis? What are the common neurotic premises about the self? What are some of the neurotic behaviours built upon these false self-concepts? Refer to the case study of John for examples of neuroticism.

3   What is schizophrenia? What are some examples of delusions in schizophrenia? How is the presence of a specific delusion shown by the schizophrenic? Why is withdrawal such a dangerous symptom of schizophrenia?

4   In what way may an over-identification with another person become a means of withdrawal from reality? How may the 'delusions of grandeur' be related to the identity problems inherent in schizophrenia? What are some common examples of hallucinations in schizophrenia?

5   How are the 'strange' experiences of the schizophrenic different from the 'supernatural' experiences of the Christian? What is the role of the family and/or Christian fellowship group to correctly communicate these differences to a client with schizophrenic tendencies?

6   Why is it so difficult to identify a sociopath, especially in a Church context? In what ways does the sociopath deceive himself and others about his 'social strengths'? How may a Christian counsellor help such a client?

CHAPTER TWELVE

Distortions of the Will

STUBBORNNESS is a trait of the will (Isaiah 48:4), but self-control is a fruit of the Spirit (Galatians 5:23). Often the will of the person becomes distorted so that the capacity to control and/or motivate behaviour in appropriate ways is lacking. Either the individual has too weak a will and can never say 'no' to specific temptations, or the person has too strong a will and tries to control circumstances in an obsessive manner. But whichever way the distortion expresses itself, the consequences are demoralising. For a person to become the slave of a thing, such as alcohol, food, sex (because of a weak will), is just as de-humanising as it is to attempt in vain to avert anxiety by ritualistic activities (because of a stubborn will).

The purpose of the will is to make decisions. If these choices are usually counter-productive, then the individual's self-confidence level will be lowered. This in turn may encourage the development of neurotic self-concepts of 'worthlessness', or it may become a chronic weakness in a character disorder. Spiritually, the Lord holds each man responsible before him because of the use (obedience) or misuse (disobedience) of the will. The overall significance of the will is summarised in Scripture in 1 Samuel 15:22, "Does the Lord delight in burnt offerings and sacrifices as much as in obeying the voice of the Lord? To obey is better than sacrifice, and to heed is better than the fat of rams."

Obsessive-compulsive Reactions

In neuroses there is often the disturbing tendency to repeat rituals that have no meaning. Compulsive actions are the meaningless acts of a will which is too strong. The strength of the will becomes obsessive, forcing the intellect to deny the meaninglessness of the ritual and the emotions almost to stop feeling. The person becomes a 'robot'. The robot-like actions are combined with obsessive thoughts, which dominate the normal thinking processes of the person. These obsessive thoughts are anxiety thoughts, usually suggesting some catastrophe or reminding the person of some past failure. The ritual-like acts become necessary as the will transfers the anxiety into action. In essence, the compulsive acts are a way of expressing the anxiety within. As the anxious thoughts get out of control then it becomes imperative to control external circumstances.

For example, a disturbing thought regarding guilt over being born may lead to the ritualistic behaviour of taking five showers a day. This was the presenting problem of a client named Rita. When she came for counselling, Rita was twenty years old, working as a typist and living alone with her mother. Rita had no friends, was unhappy with her job, but most of all upset over the showering compulsion. This compulsive act controlled the totality of her life. Rita would get up at 7.30 a.m. to shower prior to going to work; she would come home at 12.30 p.m. for shower number two; she would have her third shower at 6 p.m. after returning from work; at about 10 p.m. she would have her fourth shower prior to going to bed, and then about 3 a.m. she would awaken to take her fifth shower for the day. Because of this compulsive act, her job had to be close to home to permit a shower at lunch time, she could never visit any friends for it would mean missing a shower, and she could never even sleep through a whole night.

The origin of Rita's compulsion was the obsessive thought, "I should not have been born, now my mother's life is ruined." In fact, she had been born when her mother was just seventeen and unmarried. Rita's mother chose to keep her, abandoning instead her chance to attend a university and prepare for a teaching career. Now the mother worked part-time in a shop, devoting herself to Rita, while interjecting an occasional remark about her "lost opportunity for marriage and a career". This was a type of guilt manipulation. These remarks started early in Rita's childhood, and from an unconscious level tormented her whole psyche. The only relief was the ritual of repetitive showering. Somehow the inner feeling of guilt was 'washed away' by the external act. But because it was so short-lived a state, it had to be done again and again. Rita was a prisoner of this internalised guilt.

Rita exemplifies many of the characteristics of an obsessive-compulsive neurotic. Her behaviour was compulsive and her thoughts obsessive. Her behaviour was ritualistic but harmless — except in the way in which it restricted her life. Cleanliness rituals are common compulsions, and, as in Rita's case, often have an underlying guilt component. They become the basic outlet for the anxiety/guilt that may be repressed. Yet this very guilt, when once acknowledged, usually has a large irrational aspect. For example, Rita could not be held responsible for the circumstances of her birth, but this false (irrational) guilt was producing the obsessive thoughts. These thoughts were lies. But the lies were powerful enough to enslave her to cleanliness rituals. Her intellect believed the lies, her emotions produced the anxiety, and her will tried to control the situation via symbolic cleansing behaviour.

Eventually the will so dominates the whole psyche in an obsessive-compulsive that the behaviour cannot be stopped. But the behaviour does not reduce the anxiety either. The symbolic action becomes counter-productive, in that it produces an anxiety of its own. But still the strength of the will is supreme; the ritualistic behaviour must not stop or panic ensues. The person is indeed trapped by his own will which seeks control of the anxiety within through the external rituals. A deep feeling of helplessness, of having been unfairly manipulated and/or used (perhaps during childhood) can often strengthen the will to produce the irrational action. Even though the symbolic behaviour is rarely aggressive in nature, it is still destructive in that it erodes time, energy and the person's sense of worth.

In counselling such a person, the main concern is to discover the meaning of the compulsive behaviour. Is it motivated by guilt? If so, what aspects of the guilt are rational and what aspects are irrational? Or is there a generalised fear which motivates an obsessive desire to control something? Either guilt and/or fear are the sources of the rituals. During the counselling these two possibilities must be explored. Usually once that guilt or fear is identified, the rituals have meaning. Then the root causes of the real problem can be treated rather than just the symptoms (presenting problem). Guilt and/or fear must be brought into a realistic perspective, stripped of their inherent exaggeration and/or irrationality. Only then can the real guilt be genuinely confessed before God and man, forgiveness given, and healing be achieved. Or with fear, it is then possible to concentrate on the love of God and man at work in the client's life to reduce the fear. Specific therapeutic techniques, as discussed in Chapter Eight, can be used with specific clients after the guilt and/or fear have been correctly identified. Through supportive counselling the healing process can free the person from his own compulsive behaviour and obsessive thoughts.

Alcoholic Addiction

When the will is weak it cannot stop harmful activities from becoming addictions. The emotions of the person dominate. The focus is therefore on relieving the major feelings of anxiety. Any means available is used to reduce anxiety in the present, often without any concern over the long-term consequences of such behaviour. The will allows an impulsive act to occur, finds it reduces or covers-up the anxiety, and soon this activity overpowers the will. This is the pattern by which any addiction makes the will its slave. The specific addiction may be to food (over-eating), sex (masturbation, homosexuality, promiscuity), drugs (narcotics, amphetamines, barbiturates), gambling, stealing (kleptomania), lying (sociopathy), or drink (alcoholism). As such each of these addictions are classified as a character disorder.

Research has shown a distinctive pattern in the personality of the alcoholic. Most often he is shy, afraid of both people and of his own ability to cope with the demands of personal relationships. He is excessive in reacting to people: either another person is seen as so bad that they are in the gutter, or so good that they are on a pedestal. The 'normal' integration of strengths and weaknesses cannot be observed in others, so the alcoholic is quick to blame or to praise — often the same person at different times. Because of this, he is insensitive to others, expecting either too little or too much from a person. This means he is always disappointed in relationships, and when these expectations are not realised it leads to anger. Many alcoholics then have a dual addiction — to drink and to anger.

This interacts with another area of excessiveness — in being hurt. The alcoholic manipulates people, misjudges people and magnifies the negatives in a situation. As a consequence he is always feeling resentful/hurt. Self-pity, for not being able to adjust to these hurts, intensifies the anger toward others. Usually, projection is the outlet for this anger, as others are always to blame, or in need of changing themselves, *never* that the alcoholic is too sensitive or needs to learn how to cope with difficulties. Somewhat like a spoiled child, the alcoholic expects everything to be easy, and when it is not he sulks in self-pity and/or anger.

The third area of excessive behaviour is verbal. All potential alcoholics have an extreme oral need, which may be manifested in excessive talking, eating, smoking, nail-biting etc. For some talking equals reality; but their talk never equals their actions. So a solemn promise to stop drinking today will not be lived up to tomorrow. The fourth area of excess is in 'ego binges'. Perhaps because of the deep inferiority fears in the alcoholic, they will flaunt their abilities in a vain attempt to prove their worth. They have an excessive need to be the biggest, best, most perfect in a certain situation. The frustration is that they cannot cope with the success if they do achieve at that high level. This is why the alcoholic is sometimes called, "his majesty, the baby!"

Another definition of the alcoholic is a person who cannot cope with alcohol or without it. A common rationalisation is that with a few drinks the person is more sociable, less anxious, in essence able to cope. But this is not so. Because alcohol acts as a depressant, it slows down the functioning of the central nervous system, and deadens the person's awareness of situations and people. Thus, the presence of alcohol in the blood stream prevents adequate control of behaviour (physical addiction). Likewise, when the alcohol is absent, the person becomes so obsessed with the desire for a drink, that he cannot concentrate on anything else (psychological addiction). Either way, the alcoholic is a slave to his need to drink. As the months and the years add up, this disease continues to destroy brain cells, which makes more and more behaviours difficult to manage.

There are stages in the disease of alcoholism. Each stage is named after a letter of the Greek alphabet. Thus *alpha alcoholism* refers to heavy drinking without any loss of control over one's actions. *Beta alcoholism* is heavy drinking plus associated physical damage like cirrhosis of the liver and/or memory loss. *Gamma alcoholism* is the binge drinker who functions apparently for months without any alcohol and then goes off on a drinking binge for days and weeks. *Delta alcoholism* means continual drinking behaviour, with an associated loss of job, family and self-respect. This last type usually ends up in the total destruction of the person, in death.

Alcoholism has many symptoms (steps) which follow a particular sequence as the disease develops. Social drinking increases over a period of time until secret drinking starts. The person, motivated by shame, hides bottles of liquor in ingenious places — in a medicine bottle, in the rose bush, under the floor-board, etc. The more that secret drinking goes on, the more lies and means of concealment are necessary, all reducing the alcoholic's self-respect. Another symptom, blackouts, may then occur. Essentially, blackouts are a temporary state of amnesia, in which the alcoholic 'functions' but has not the memory of his activity. During such a blackout an alcoholic may go to another city, commit a crime, get married, or swim the English Channel — all without any awareness of what was done! However, the fear of having done something, and hence being responsible for an act that is unknown, haunts the alcoholic. The most dramatic symptom of alcoholism is the DT's. Delirium tremens affect only a small percentage of all alcoholics, but the presence of uncontrollable shaking and tactile/visual hallucinations (bugs crawling on the skin, telephone wires turning into snakes), reinforces the reality of needing help! These DT's are withdrawal symptoms which may be minimised by giving the alcoholic a drink. The danger is that once the hallucinations are over, the alcoholic is no longer motivated to get treatment.

Counselling of alcoholics can be difficult because of their inconsistent motivation to change. Three principles for treating the alcoholic must be followed. First, the person must honestly admit that he is "powerless over alcohol". The will cannot function to control the addiction. Resolutions to reform cannot last, they only give false hopes to everyone concerned. But when an admission of desperation is given, and the person is 'willing to be willing' to let Christ take over his life — then healing of the person begins. Only the power of the Lord is strong enough to break the power of physical and psychological dependency on alcohol. Secondly, the cycle of anger/resentment/self-pity must be confronted in the person as a cause of the problem. At Alcoholics Anonymous, this is referred to as a 'Self-inventory' of strength and weaknesses that can be used to counteract the rightness of resentment. The person must learn to be responsible for his own behaviour and feelings, which means unlearning past rationalisations and projections. This may take a long time, with many slips backward into old thinking patterns and self-pity reactions. But it can be done with a new dependence upon God for patience to strengthen the will to persevere. Thirdly, the alcoholic client needs peer-group support to maintain both sobriety and emotional growth.

Since alcoholism is a disease, the real problem is arrested not cured; and this means that any relapse into drinking continues the disease process from the very point where it was left before. But the peer group, preferably with some former alcoholics in it, can put pressure on the client to stay sober "one day at a time". Peer pressure can also prevent the client from diverting the addictive tendencies into another outlet, such as gambling or over-eating. For these reasons, it is often advisable to have the alcoholic client as part of a group counselling context. Or if this is not possible, to have a close-knit fellowship group within the Church which would be able to support the alcoholic, both spiritually and emotionally.

There should be opportunities in the Church to educate the Christian concerning alcoholism (Proverbs 23:29-35). Then the Christian counsellor will be better prepared to deal with the problem and the Church as a whole to encourage the person.

The Compulsive Eater

Gluttony is the biblical word for the psychological problem of over-eating. This is not simply a problem of obesity, since not all over-eaters are fat, but rather an example of a will too weak to control normal hunger responses.

From the earliest weeks of life, there is an association between love and food learned by the child. Whenever the infant is hungry, he is picked up and loved while being fed. So the two needs, for love and food, are satisfied together. Throughout life this inherent association continues; that is why the adult who is deprived of love will often over-eat as compensation. Any type of deprivation, with an implied loss of a loved object or person, can set up a binge of over-eating. From simply not getting one's own way in an argument to the grief reaction for a dead spouse, each frustration can focus the attention on the loss of love and/or self-esteem. This agony is very conscious, but the giving to oneself of food (usually sweets and starches) can literally sugar-coat the hurt. Physiologically there is then satisfaction. This reduction in physical tension may generalise to the psychological domain. Anxiety may also be reduced.

This approach to coping with anxiety sets up a cycle of dependency on food which traps the person. The over-eater is anxious so he eats more, but soon becomes angry at not being able to stop eating which makes him even more anxious. Various means of trying to control this cycle show the desperation of the person — such as self-enforced vomiting or fad diets. The will of the person is strong enough to force such extreme reactions to over-eating, but it is never strong enough to stop the gluttony. Why? Because some need for love and/or attention is still being met by the over-eating itself.

This compulsive oral activity of over-eating may have other root causes similar to those of alcoholism. Some resentment, self-pity and an extreme desire to control situations according to one's own rules — may each contribute to the compulsion.

For girls, especially in their teens and twenties, over-eating may be a defence against sexual involvements. These young women put a layer of fat between them and the world, as an extra 'protection' against the possibility of some male finding them attractive. Their fear of sex forces them to deny their femininity, and allows them to feel 'ugly'. This same fear of sex joined to an oral impregnation fantasy may produce in a young girl the opposite behavioural symptom of compulsive fasting (anorexia nervosa). With an anorexic client, starvation is a real possibility, yet she is never conscious of being hungry. The will is too weak to force any food down, because it is dominated by an irrational fear of pregnancy and/or sex. If there is already a neurotic self-concept of 'worthlessness', then being 'ugly' or 'skinny' can help to strengthen it. For young men, over-eating may be a defence against other types of presumed inferiority, such as shyness, stupidity, and over-sensitivity. Usually the obese young person is not good at sport activities, must dress in non-fashionable ways, and generally feels too 'big' to fit in comfortably at social functions. Depression as well as neurotic feelings of inferiority can result from compulsive eating, or vice-versa.

In counselling a compulsive eater, it is imperative to distinguish symptom from cause. More often the over-eating is but a symptom of depression, neuroses, or a substitute for alcohol. Yet this symptom is serious enough to disrupt the psychological health of the person, and as such must be treated. Many of the counselling principles to use with alcoholics would apply. In the United States the A.A. programme has been slightly adapted to form O.A. (Over-eaters Anonymous). Finding other means of satisfying frustrations/anger and having peer pressure to promote abstinence — are each essential in counselling an over-eater. Since body image always affects self-concept, it is the client's view (usually unrealistic) of self that must be identified and then corrected.

As strengths within the personality grow, the person believes more in his worth before God, and the will begins to control the eating behaviour. When the will becomes stronger, it in turn strengthens the self-esteem of the person. This becomes a healthy cycle within the psyche. The client changes from being a slave to compulsion to being a freed son/daughter of God (John 12:46).

Points for Discussion

1   How may a will become too strong or too weak to produce 'normality' within the personality? What is the role of the will in making a person responsible before God?

2   What is an obsessive-compulsive reaction? Identify the major symptoms, and the role of the will in producing them. Refer to the case study of Rita to show the behaviour of an obsessive-compulsive person.

3   What approach may a Christian counsellor use to help an obsessive-compulsive client? How may the guilt and/or fear be dealt with by the counsellor?

4   What would be an acceptable definition of alcoholism? What are some of the alcoholic's personality traits which contribute to his drinking behaviour? How may his problem be identified before its disease properties destroy him?

5   What are the different types of alcoholism? Which type is
     easier to identify and which type is easier to treat? What
     should be the role of the peer groups and the family in the
     successful treatment of an alcoholic? Why is there a danger
     that the 'arrested' alcoholic may suddenly become a
     gambler?

6   What apparently motivates the compulsive eater to con-
     tinue to eat even when this produces self-hatred too? How
     may an irrational self-concept (especially in adolescents)
     contribute to either a problem of anorexia or over-eating?

7   How may a Christian counsellor support and/or correct
     the intellect of a compulsive eater?

APPENDIX
The Major Psychological Disorders

A. Neuroses — An inability to cope with reality problems

1   This is the most common type of emotional disturbance, shown mostly in a *distortion* of oneself or the situation in an attempt to cope with problems.

2   There is usually an underlying sense of inferiority and/or guilt, even to the extreme of feeling *worthless* as the anxiety develops within the person.

3   **Main types:**   anxiety reaction.
                          obsessive compulsive reactions.
                          neurotic depression.
                          phobias.

4   **Usual outcome:**   good care and counsel needed during intense periods of anxiety and/or fears.

5   **Main symptoms:**   anxiety shown in either inferiority or superiority attitudes.

6   **Counselling aim:** Listen — giving support to the person and a clarification of real problem.

B. Psychoses — An inability to recognise or relate properly to people or things in the environment.

1   This is the most serious type of mental illness, shown mostly in a denial of aspects of oneself or the situation, and a substitution of fantasy (delusional) ideas and even hallucinations (hearing voices, seeing images etc.).

2   There is often an underlying biological and/or hereditary component to this illness, which makes medical treatment necessary for the person.

3   **Main types:**   schizophrenia.
                          psychotic depression.

4	Usual outcome:	guarded; depends on availability of appropriate treatment.
5	Main symptoms:	delusions (false beliefs) shown in unusual patterns of thinking, feeling and acting; and a withdrawal from reality/people.
6	Counselling aim:	Listen — giving support to the person and suggesting medical referrals for further treatment.

C. Character Disorders — An inability to control one part or dimension of behaviour.

1   This is an exaggeration of the most common weaknesses in human beings. Examples are *compulsive* eating, drinking (alcoholism), gambling, killing, stealing, sexual distortions (homosexuality, promiscuity), lying, and drug related dependencies.

2   There is usually an underlying habitual pattern which has lasted for many years. On the surface the person may have seemed to be improving (e.g. stop drinking) only to become involved in another compulsion (e.g. drug addiction or gambling).

3	Main types:	Sociopathy. Alcoholism.
4	Usual outcome:	guarded; depends on the motivation of the person to change and the support given to encourage this change.
5	Main symptoms:	habitual personality weaknesses shown in compulsive behaviours.
6	Counselling aim:	Listen — giving support to the person and confronting him with his own types of self-deceptions.

Bibliography

Secular Psychology and Counselling Approaches

Caplan, Gerald. *Principles of Preventive Psychiatry* (New York: Basic Books, 1964).

Erikson, Eric H. *Childhood and Society* (New York: Norton, 1963).

Glasser, William. *Reality Therapy* (New York: Harper and Row, 1960).

Rogers, Carl R. *Client-centred Therapy* (Boston: Houghton-Mifflin Co., 1951).

Sheehy, Gail G. *Passages: Predictable Crisis of Adult Life* (New York: Bantam Books, 1977).

Christian Psychology and Counselling Approaches

Adams, Jay E. *The Christian Counselor's Manual* (Philadelphia, Pa: Presbyterian and Reformed Publishing Co., 1973).

Collins, Gary. *The Rebuilding of Psychology: An Integration of Psychology and Christianity* (Wheaton, Ill: Tyndale House, 1977).

Cosgrove, Mark and Mallory, James. *Mental Health: A Christian Approach* (Grand Rapids, Mich: Zondervan Publishing House, 1977).

Crabb, Larry. *Effective Biblical Counselling* (Grand Rapids, Mich: Zondervan Publishing House, 1977).

Hyder, O. Quentin. *The Christian's Handbook of Psychiatry* (Old Tappan, N. J.: Revell, 1971).

Hyder, O. Quentin. *The People You Live With* (Old Tappan, N.J.: Revell, 1975).

Lloyd-Jones, Martyn. *Spiritual Depression* (Glasgow: Pickering and Inglis Ltd, 1965).

Mallory, James. *The Kink and I: A Psychiatrist's Guide to Untwisted Living* (Wheaton, Ill: Victor Books, 1973).

Miller, William A. *Why do Christians Break Down?* (London: Coverdale House, 1974).

Stapleton, Ruth C. *The Gift of Inner Healing* (London: Hodder and Stoughton, 1977).

Tournier, Paul. *A Doctor's Casebook in the Light of the Bible* (New York: Harper and Row, 1960).

Index